meiji japan's centennial:
aspects of political thought and action

Studies on Asia, Second Series (Volume I—1968)
Grant K. Goodman, General Editor

Midwest Conference on Asian Affairs

RELEASED

meiji japan's centennial:
aspects of political thought and action

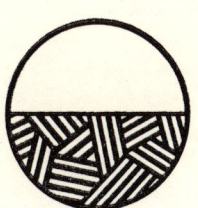

DS
2
.S8
2d ser.
vol. 1

Edited by David Wurfel

154731

THE UNIVERSITY PRESS OF KANSAS/LAWRENCE/MANHATTAN/WICHITA

© Copyright 1971 by the University Press of Kansas
Standard Book Number 7006-0076-0
Library of Congress Catalog Card Number 79-148953
Designed by Fritz Reiber
Printed in the United States of America

EDITOR'S PREFACE

It is a great pleasure and a high honor for me as General Editor of *Studies on Asia, Second Series* to introduce this distinguished collection of scholarly papers. All of them were first presented at the 1968 meeting of the Midwest Conference on Asian Affairs. The Conference Executive Committee, with the support of the entire Conference, having committed itself to begin to publish again *Studies on Asia,* this time under the imprint of the University Press of Kansas, and having decided to produce annual volumes on specific, central themes, was fortunate not only to commence this new venture in the Meiji centennial year but also to attract contributions from such careful and thoughtful scholars as those whose pieces compose this volume. Much of the credit for the high caliber of this compilation must go to my indefatigable co-editor, Professor David Wurfel, who worked in complete harmony with me in all of the editorial tasks which, while minimally visible in the finished product, are nevertheless time consuming in the utmost.

Grant K. Goodman
University of Kansas

INTRODUCTION

The seventeenth annual Midwest Conference on Asian Affairs—held at Western Michigan University in Kalamazoo, fell in the hundredth year since the boy-emperor Mutsuhito, in a Kyoto ceremony, chose the reign name Meiji, marking the onset of a period of rapid change in Japanese society. It was thus appropriate to use this centennial, a time for celebrations, commemorative publication, and historical controversy in Japan, as the focus of the 1968 Conference program. Not all the papers presented dealt with Japan and the Meiji era, but the best of those that did have been gathered together in this volume.

We were very fortunate in having as our keynote speaker at Kalamazoo—whose lecture then became the first selection within these covers—one of the leading specialists in Japanese history, Professor Marius Jansen of Princeton University. Professor Jansen paints in broad strokes, but with the sure hand of a master calligrapher, the character of and causes for change in the Meiji period. In his comments on the pattern of change, now usually referred to as modernization, he focuses on the nature of leadership and on the context in which these leaders worked.

Professor Jansen reminds us that despite the comparative orderliness of Japan's rapid transformation, there was much confusion. Confusion extended from feudal rulers to peasants when they were confronted with new institutions, new roles to play, and new patterns of power. Some were so frustrated by this confusion that they sought to restore important aspects of the old order by destroying the most "objectionable" representatives of the new. Professor Jansen points out that these opponents of change more often became popular heroes than did the major leaders of the Restoration. Thus prominent assassins often gained widespread sympathy and even respect.

Professor Sidney Brown of the Department of History of Oklahoma State University describes in some detail in his contribution one of the most important assassinations in the Meiji era, and the public reaction to it. The assassins were in the tradition of the *shishi,* self-styled "men of high purpose," who were usually ex-samurai. Loyalty, duty, courage, and daring were their watchwords; direct action was their style. While such men directed their attack against the shogunate in its last days, after the Meiji Restoration their commitment was to the old order. In both eras they acted in the name of the emperor.

Professor Jansen has pointed out some of the continuities in Japanese life from Meiji to the present. In that spirit it might be appropriate to suggest a link all the way from the feudal swordsmen who cut down the home minister in 1878 to the student revolutionists of today. The link with contemporary rightists is more obvious, but despite their very different goals, even the neo-Marxist-anarchist in Tokyo today seems to share something of the *shishi* style. Courage in action, devotion to an "ideologically" defined duty, and loyalty to fellow conspirators are at least as important as the ultimate objective, often only dimly viewed.

Professor Barbara Teters, of the Department of Political Science of Iowa State University, has contributed a chapter which describes a different type of assassin, in no sense a popular hero, and in this case unsuccessful in his attempt on the life of the visiting Romanov crown prince, Nicholas. This instance reminds us that such acts of violence against key figures have more than once been used by Japanese who wanted to change the direction of their nation's foreign policy. (There was, therefore, a very sound basis for the decision to cancel President Eisenhower's trip to Japan in 1960.)

Professor Teters' paper concentrates more, however, on the impact of this incident on Japanese judicial practice than on the motivation or fate of the assassin. Thanks to the forceful personality and firm convictions of the chief justice of the supreme court, the catalyst of an assassin's daring did not erode, but actually strengthened, a judicial system which, at least in its higher reaches, was struggling for independence from political intervention. In this piece on the Otsu Jiken, Professor Teters is more impressed with the order than with the disorder in this stage of Japanese modernization.

The two subsequent pieces in this volume concern the impact of Meiji Japan abroad. Much has been written about Japanese expansionism in the Meiji era. That is certainly one of the less happy aspects of this remarkable period, an aspect which receives more attention from Japanese than from American scholars. But here, in pioneering research in original sources, Professor Frank Wong, Department of History, Antioch College, and Professor E. Thadeus Flood of the Department of History of the University of Santa Clara have described aspects of the spill-over of Meiji Japan into Asia.

Professor Wong's chapter discusses the significance of the Meiji constitution for Ch'ing reformers in Peking. Despite the close study the Chinese made of the Japanese polity—remarkable in itself for a people accustomed to being Japan's cultural creditor, not debtor—Meiji-style reforms were not effected in China in time to save the throne. In fact, the attempt to do so in The Hundred Days was overturned by the backward-looking empress dowager. It is doubtful, however, whether the empire would have survived even if the Japanese model had been faithfully followed. Professor Jansen's stress, in his essay, on the favorable context in explaining the "successes" of the Meiji period seems to point up the "failures" in the case of China.

In the midst of speculation today about whether the Japanese pattern of modernization is applicable to Asia's many "late-starters," it is well to remember that even in the late nineteenth century, when it was most relevant, it was not emulated. Professor Wong points out that despite considerable knowledge of Japanese experience, Chinese officials interpreted what they learned in terms of their own stake in the regime. Thus the reforms finally instituted in the twilight of the Ch'ing dynasty were something less than sweeping.

Thailand, like China, had an ancient monarchy reeling from the blows of Western impact. She did not have the degree of contact with Japan that China did, however. She did not share a cultural tradition, nor was she threatened by Japan's remarkable military ascendancy. Furthermore, by learning directly from the West, the Thai under King Mongkut had begun the modernization process even before the accomplishments of the Meiji era became known to them. It is not surprising, therefore, that Professor Flood, despite extensive research in Thai archives, has found no evidence that Bangkok reformers saw Japan as their model.

This is not because the Thai were ignorant of Japanese developments. Like the Chinese, they sent a constitutional study mission to Tokyo. They also became aware of the enterprising Meiji spirit through the escapades of ex-samurai adventurers. This Professor Flood calls Thailand's *"shishi* interlude." In an excess of zeal and a dearth of planning or common sense, the *shishi* failed miserably in their efforts to establish Japanese agricultural colonies in Thailand. Despite some financial backing in both Japan and Bangkok, persistent failure dried up even this support. Though preaching Pan-Asianism and anti-Westernism, the adventurers did not strike a sympathetic chord in the Thai elite, who remained very open to Western influences.

Returning to the *shishi*—where we began in Professor Brown's research—we are reminded that they influenced not only the style of later domestic politics but that of foreign policy as well. There are striking parallels, for instance, in the attitudes of the nineteenth-century *shishi* in Thailand and of the more idealistic proponents of the Greater East Asia Co-prosperity Sphere;

e.g., Colonel Suzuki, who led the Burma Independence Army in 1941. This is, of course, no hoary plot, but simply a common thread in outlook and behavior of one type of Japanese.

This collection of studies on Meiji Japan was originally undertaken in connection with the aforementioned centennial. As Professor Jansen points out, the centennial itself, as well as the meaning of the Meiji Restoration, has been a subject of great controversy in Japan.* Present-day ideological commitments cause scholars to raise the basic issue whether Japan's history is triumph or shame, something to be honored or scorned. The counterestablishment suspects the government of using the Meiji centenary to glorify the past in order to build support for conservative policies.

American scholars would certainly prefer to simply note that 1968 is one hundred years after 1868 and to stay clear of this argument. But the American viewpoint has itself become a subject of debate. In fact, many more than the Marxist scholars in Japan criticize American historians for painting too bright a picture of Japan's modernization. Too little attention, it is said, is paid to the dark side, the violence, the human costs of Japan's progress. Some Americans would counter that Japanese intel-

---

* For a fuller discussion see John W. Hall, "Reflections on a Centennial," *Journal of Asian Studies*, XXVII: 4 (August 1968), 711-20.

lectuals often appear to be congenital pessimists, reluctant to give fair weight to the good alongside the bad.

And yet there may be some validity in the Japanese scholars' critique. Even if there is, however, it can hardly be applied to this volume. While none of us would deny the remarkable achievements of the Meiji era, of which Professor Jansen takes note, the studies here remind the reader of the persistence of certain feudal values and thus of the unevenness of progress. Some American scholars—especially those who are not Japan specialists—may be so impressed with Japan's ability to maintain internal order during spectacular economic growth that they would subtly suggest to today's modernizers in Asia that Japan is worthy of emulation. The last two papers of *this* volume have described two cases in which the "Japanese model" was not followed. Yet China and Thailand were the only other independent monarchies in Asia at the turn of the century, those polities in which the Meiji reforms would seem to have been most applicable.

This volume makes no pretense at grand theory or at dramatic new discovery. Nor can any work of diverse authorship hope to be entirely consistent in its interpretations. But if American scholars have ever been guilty of over-selling Meiji accomplishments, the error is not repeated here.

David Wurfel
University of Windsor

CONTENTS

EDITOR'S PREFACE
Grant K. Goodman   v

INTRODUCTION
David Wurfel   vi

THE MEIJI RESTORATION
Marius B. Jansen   2

POLITICAL ASSASSINATION IN EARLY MEIJI JAPAN: THE PLOT AGAINST ŌKUBO TOSHIMICHI
Sidney DeVere Brown   18

THE OTSU AFFAIR: THE FORMATION OF JAPAN'S JUDICIAL CONSCIENCE
Barbara Teters   36

THE MEIJI MODEL AND CHINESE CONSTITUTIONAL REFORMERS
Frank F. Wong   64

THE SHISHI INTERLUDE IN OLD SIAM: AN ASPECT OF THE MEIJI IMPACT IN SOUTHEAST ASIA
E. Thadeus Flood   78

meiji japan's centennial:
aspects of political thought and action

The Meiji Restoration

Marius B. Jansen
Princeton University

A century ago Japan was weak, divided, unstable, and poor. Its leaders were conscious of the fact that Japan was well behind much of the Western world, and they were convinced that political reorganization and centralization were urgently needed to close the gap. Two feudal baronies agreed on a general proposal for change which they argued in this language:

"Our first great duty is to seek out the national polity and structure of the Imperial Country of old so that we may face all nations without shame. For that purpose we must restore Imperial rule and study to establish an order of government within the land, of such a nature that future generations will not regret our actions." After laying out the evils of decentralization, they went on to deplore the fact that, as a result of the feudal divisions, "some do not even realize that there is an Emperor. When one thinks about this with the world in mind, is there anywhere else a national polity like this? It is evident that we must reform our regulations and return political power to the court, form a council of feudal lords, and conduct affairs in line with the desires of the people as expressed in this manner; only then can we face all nations without shame and establish our national polity."[1]

There is here a self-conscious contrast between Japan and the outside world; one notes the urgent need to centralize around the emperor, the intention to consult opinion broadly, and a determination to create something for which future generations will not need to feel shame. The Charter Oath of the Meiji Emperor, issued in April 1868, continued these aims: a council chamber to be established; all classes to achieve their just aspiration; wisdom to be sought throughout the world; and absurd customs of the past to be discarded. And all this so that the foundations of the empire might be established and made firm.

Looked at from the vantage of a century, we have to agree that these goals were achieved. It is true that a few decades ago Japanese did indeed feel shame, a shame greater even than their grandfathers knew, but that too is past. In recent decades all classes have certainly achieved their just aspirations, absurd customs have been discarded, and the foundations of the empire have never seemed more firm. Japan stands as one of the world's great powers in all the ways that count, and represents, after the United States, the Soviet Union, and all of Western Europe, the largest potential of productive power in the world. In the 1870's Japanese voyagers to Europe still felt themselves a half century behind the West. But in the 1960's Japanese travelers found their technology superior to that of Europe. A recent series of reflections by the sociologist Katō Hidetoshi concludes that Japan and the United States, alone in the world, have passed through modernization into what he calls "contemporary society"; one characterized by a high-mobility, mass-consumption society, its tastes and desires regulated by mass media, and its members dedicated to constant, and upward, motion.[2]

Japan's century of change ought to provide a variety of conclusions and reflections on the course and pace of modernization. Some have general applicability for modern histories everywhere, but most take us back to the distinctive social and cultural patterns within Japan itself.

October 23, 1968, was the official centennial of the event that has been taken to mark the beginning of modern Japan. A century earlier the boy-emperor Mutsuhito reached for a sacred lot in a Shinto ceremony and selected a slip. It bore the Chinese characters "bright" and "rule," selected from *The Book of Changes*; read together they make "Meiji," designating the year or era of "enlightened rule" that would extend until the emperor's death in 1912. I have used the same language in "The Meiji State," p. 95 in James B. Crowley, ed., *Modern East Asia: Essays in Interpretation* (New York, 1970). The decree which announced the change in designation of the era made clear that thereafter there would be only one era name per sovereign. History would now enroll in emperor-sized units, instead of being divided into eras set off at the discretion of the government in accordance with numerological wisdom. Thus a development that began in China with the Ming dynasty in 1368, one that signified the final stage in imperial absolutism, came to Japan in

1868. Not war, or even defeat and a new beginning in 1945, would require a new year designation. All that counted was the continuity of imperial rule.

A few weeks before this the court had renamed the feudal capital from Edo to Eastern Capital, Tokyo. In November the boy-emperor set out on a visit to his new capital. A procession of three thousand men had at its center the great palanquin in which he sat. It was topped by a phoenix, and carried by a swarm of yellow-robed bearers. He was a full six feet above the ground, and upon the approach of this strange conveyance, a contemporary reporter tells us, "a great silence fell upon the people. Far as the eye could see on either side, the roadsides were densely packed with the crouching populace. And as the phoenix car with its halo of glittering attendants came on . . . the people without order or signal turned their faces to the earth. No man moved or spoke for a space, and all seemed to hold their breath for very awe, as the mysterious presence, on whom few are privileged to look and live, was passing by."[3]

Thus modern Japan came into being with silence and awe, rather than with noise and celebration. It is true that fighting came before this, and continued after it. The shogun's vassals thought, quite correctly, that he had been cheated and double-crossed, and that the early terms on which he was asked to surrender his powers had been forgotten in the eagerness to get at his lands and wealth. The entry into Tokyo was an act of psychological and political warfare that accompanied the military campaigns against his followers, a civil war that came to an end only in the early summer of 1869. And there was some celebration as well, not least because the emperor's visit to Tokyo was accompanied by free distribution of *sake* as an expression of imperial benevolence.

But most of all there was confusion. The certainties of long centuries of a structured and stratified feudal society were soon in process of change, but the nature and degree of that change were far from clear. Uncertainty extended from the ranks of the feudality to the peasants. The feudal lords were not sure how things would come out, shocked by the sudden revelation of shogunal weakness and uncomfortable about their own pledges and role. Most of them sat it out and left the fighting to a few diehard Tokugawa vassals and an equally few ambitious southwestern fiefs whose leaders styled themselves the emperor's army. Many assumed another war would follow among the winners,

5

and one group of allies had a full set of plans ready to make off with the emperor in the event of such a war so that they could not end up on the "disloyal" side. Even after the war was over the feudal lords were uncertain how to behave in the new order. How did one live his life without the ritual decorum established during the years of feudal status? We find one baron sending in a remarkably detailed set of questions to the new government: Should he go to restaurants or not? If he does, can he call for singing girls? Is it all right to call them to his residence? If he heads for the licensed quarter with his men, should he do so openly or even secretly? "At this time of innovation," he explains, "we would like to know the correct way to conduct ourselves."[4]

Some, even among the leaders, never found how to conduct themselves. Yōdō, lord of Tosa, troubled in his conscience and contemptuous of his associates among the Restoration daimyo, went on a collosal drunk that scandalized his retainers and killed him a few years later at the age of 45.[5] But most others, burdened with debts and grateful to be relieved of their responsibilities, accepted appointment as governors of their fiefs, then accepted bonds in place of feudal revenues, and finally, in 1884, patents of nobility in a new, European-style peerage. One finds their descendants today in all walks of life. A very few are elected governors of the areas their ancestors ruled. Others hold posts of social honor in the Red Cross, museums, or similar organizations; but most, with the abolition of the peerage and the land reform that followed World War II, have disappeared into the urban throng.

Ordinary samurai were no less confused. Those who had fled their lords to fight for the imperial cause, and whose intrigues and free-wheeling activism had helped create the ferment of change, were told that though their activities were much appreciated and "It is owing not a little to their ability of taking initiative that the Imperial Court has come to be restored to power again," the time for free wheeling was at an end. "Now all policies are to be decided by the Emperor Himself. It is hoped that those who had previously left their clans will return to their original prefectures, properly registered, abide with faith and justice, mind their conduct, and cooperate with and assist the Government."[6] The revolution is over, gentlemen, thank you very much. And so the samurai were gradually deprived of their incomes, swords, and privileges. First they were reclassified into two major groups instead of the multiple military ranks in which they had been arrayed. Five years later, plans for universal manhood conscription signaled an end to their monopoly of violence, and at the same time a graduated pension system took them off the tax rolls in what it was hoped would be easy steps toward self-reliance and support. Within a decade they were forbidden to carry the swords that had been their insignia of class. Many, of course, were needed to run the new government, and they staffed it at all levels. But the rationalization of administration that resulted from making fifty prefectures out of some 300 fiefs, each of which had had its own bureaucracy, put most of them out of business and many of them into poverty. Where expectations were the highest, in the southwestern domains that had led the restoration, a crescendo of rebellions culminated in the great Satsuma revolt of 1877. Long thereafter samurai relief was an important consideration in economic and political planning.

And what of the commoners who crouched along the roadside as the phoenix car carrying the emperor was carried along? Their confusion and fears were scarcely less. Perhaps fortunately for Japan, and certainly for the new government, their expectations were few and their participation slight. Discipline and order remained intact. Still, the substitution of new for familiar forms of rule produced sporadic distress and nearly 200 local rebellions or protests within the first decade. Some were based on groundless fears, some on resistance to change, some on local and specific outrage, and some represented revolutionary discontent. But overall there is no reason to question Thomas Smith's assertion that the lack of a revolution from below permitted the government to institute a revolution from above; that the aristocrats could be revolutionary because they did not have to look behind them.[7] And so the commoners soon found themselves with the dignity of family names; with rights of occupancy, sale, and residence of land; and blessed with rights and duties of education and conscription. In the future they would follow their emperor and fight for him, instead of being fought over and crouching by the roadside in silence while their betters swaggered by.

A centennial provides an opportunity to remember the past and to think about its significance. In the case of the Meiji centennial, it is particularly interesting to examine its leadership, its setting, and its significance for Japanese since Meiji.

Marius B. Jansen

Leadership

As Japan looks back on the Restoration, the printed page and television screen are full of reminders of the heroism that accompanied it. The individual figures who struck out against their normal bonds of loyalty and duty get the praise. The story is full of reminders of the insecurity and weakness that Japan felt a century ago in the face of a world dominated by maritime imperialist giants. There is much talk of the wisdom or fortune of the decisions made and plans carried out by men who begin to seem larger, and wiser, and stronger than life. The poignancy of this recollection is the sharper for the quickness of the recollection that two decades ago Japan was again weak, defenseless, and defeated in its confrontation with the powers it had tried to challenge. And yet it somehow has been able to regain, almost overnight, its standing as one of the world's great powers.

The significance of the Meiji Restoration, we now can see, is that it marked the emergence of a *modernizing elite,* a group firmly committed to the goals of making of their backward country a modern nation state. Their goals were expressed in terms of the models of which they had knowledge: the capitalist, representative, dynamic, industrial, and maritime powers of the Atlantic world. Negatively their goals were fixed by the misfortunes of their immediate neighbors in China, where resistance to change had brought defeat, humiliation, and disunity. Instinctively their thoughts of unity and strength were formulated around the figure of the imperial symbol, a remembered good and a viable alternative to feudal disunity. A new idea is almost always easier to explain in terms of an old one, and the phoenix car carrying the boy emperor had the multiple symbolism of rebirth and return, restoration and reform, mystery and majesty, festival and force. The car could be related to every portable shrine carried through a festive village crowd by chanting youths: heavy, but light upon the multitude of backs that support it; awesome, but not of substance. And so the Meiji Emperor provides a permanent subject of interest for the student of Japanese history and psychology; used but deeply venerated and loved by his ministers, popular but remote from his people, and in his maturity a believable, somewhat crusty sovereign who expressed opinions only to have them set aside out of greater deference to his authority. Deified in death, he is also venerated in memory, and the centennial program is centered about his name and figure. Books, museums, statues, halls, parks, and forests spring up on every hand, and from life insurance to chocolate there is no better name.

The real leaders, the true modernizers, were the little group of men from the southwestern fiefs who designed the new state structure. The seven of them who survived to become genro averaged twenty-five years of age at the time of the Restoration.[8] They were samurai of middling rank, experienced in administration and leadership but barred from real power in the old system. They were aware of the power of the West, several through personal experience of it, but able to resist the characterization of being overtly pro-West or Western specialists. They were instead pro-Japanese, able to abandon an initial position of alliance with Japan's Asian neighbors in favor of an understanding with the West, and ultimately to join with the West at the cost of China and Korea. They were pragmatists, not ideologists, who recognized and spoke the language of power. In the world they knew the sinews of power were those of iron and steel, in railroads, factories, and warships. A people trained to use these through education and conscription, trained to participate through representation, and guided by imperial pronouncements about loyalty and patriotism was the guarantee of national survival.

Although some outshine the others, no one of this group could be permitted to obscure the greater glory of the Meiji Emperor. One looks in vain for Yamagata squares or streets, or Itō parks. True, there is an Itō statue, and his image is on the paper money. But the heroes of the process seem less those who made the grade, and who need no sympathy, than those who failed or those who resisted bravely the erosion of the old feudal bonds. Saigō Takamori, who led the last great samurai revolt in 1877, comes in for much more praise and evaluation than does Itō. The historian Takeuchi Yoshimi has said that Saigō's values and goals centered after all on man, his character and his happiness; while Itō's and Ōkubo's lay with the state and its power. For the one the state was a means, for the other it was the end-all.[9] The commemoration of the Meiji centennial has focused as much on the tragedy and the failures as on the success and the result. Television serials recount the lives of those who strove and died, like Sakamoto Ryōma, more than those who lived to lead, like Yamagata Aritomo.

There are a number of reasons for this. One is the lament

that noble spirits did not survive to affect the later history that was dominated by hardheaded pragmatists. There is also the appeal of the idealism and universalism of values of the Tokugawa men, a generation educated and grounded in a selfless, Confucian cult of loyalty. Thus Japanese long accustomed to think in terms of the Meiji goals of wealth and strength see something new in the instructions Yokoi Shōnan, who fell to an assassin's sword, gave his nephew when he left to study at Rutgers: "Do not restrict your goals to national wealth and national strength, but proclaim the great purpose—*taigi*—throughout the world."[10] This is somehow more satisfying, and moving, than the Meiji acceptance of the hierarchy of civilized countries, and Aoki Shūzō's exclamation that with the revision of the treaties in 1894 "Japan has joined the ranks of civilized countries!" So the centennial evokes thoughts of what might have been as well as of what was.

Still, in the Meiji group that led there is enough to praise and examine. Through common origin, restricted numbers, and shared experience, they developed an extraordinary ability to work, and disagree, and nevertheless cooperate in the face of challenge or danger. Stability and continuity of purpose have rarely been more evident in a group of founding fathers. Most of them went abroad for eighteen months a mere four years after the Restoration, and came back to find their jobs waiting for them. Evidently they respected each other's feelings in defeat, and concealed their own exultation in success. One recognizes them in the village councils our social scientists describe.[11] There, too, men have learned to work together for a very long period of time, and for some of the same reasons; a consciousness of the importance of the group and the collectivity of belonging and representing, rather than owning and disposing, and an awareness that cooperation will be necessary again tomorrow.

The Meiji leaders, with their agreement on goals of modernization, tended to share power. It is true that in specialized bureaucracies like the army a Yamagata built up prolonged tenure and personal power. But in the more visible posts the rotation and balance between factions came almost to resemble the monthly alternation—*tsukiban*—of Tokugawa administrative practice, and led to the natural and rather innocent question of the emperor during a council to select a new prime minister: "Why don't you just take turns?"[12]

No doubt there were many reasons for this. Jealousy and

rivalry were present. No one man or faction could dominate. There seems to have been considerable reluctance and distaste for the confinement of administrative responsibility, particularly on the part of a man like Itō. And with maturity, each of the surviving oligarchs tended to become the center of a little hierarchy of his own, a little emperor, his influence extended (as Ishida Takeshi once put it) by retainers who professed to speak for him. At this stage, influence almost seems proportional to inaction.

Whatever the cause, the modernizing oligarchy made no attempt to pereptuate itself. This is worth some comment, for they sprang from a patriarchal, hereditary class. It is true that they had risen in protest against its inefficiencies. It is also true that much of the modern world of which they gained knowledge was moving in an opposite direction, but not, of course, all of it. In fact some of the Germans who helped devise the Meiji constitution assumed that Japan would have both a working emperor and a self-perpetuating aristocracy in the successors to the oligarchs they knew. But neither came to pass. The original group averaged 73 years of age, but the last of them died in 1924. If one includes Saionji, then the last of the group died in 1940, but only the crises of the 1930's brought Saionji back to prominence. Why was there so little lineal succession? One might mention Makino or Kido Kōichi. But almost without exception the oligarchs performed their last service by failing to provide powerful progeny. The abolition of the peerage after World War II ended even ceremonial honors, and today one finds their heirs scattered throughout society, sometimes in universities, and certainly far from power.

Most of Japanese society and tradition reinforced this aversion to individual eminence. The nail that sticks out, as the proverb has it, is hammered down. The collectivity has its demands. But it is particularly true that in politics nothing could be allowed to seem to overshadow the emperor. This was true even in the dynamic 1930's, when no fascist type of leader could emerge. And today, in milder form, we ses it in the assumption of Liberal-Democrat party faction leaders that they should have a fair chance to share power. In the Meiji period the entire apparatus of behind-the-scenes consensus tended to make prolonged stays in power unlikely. Recent studies by Akita and Najita show how jumpy Yamagata became if someone seemed to be getting too well entrenched in the Prime Minister's office. Everything worked for rotation. Seen in length of cabinets, the story is one of constant change; but seen in consistency of incumbents and continuity of purpose, it is one of remarkable continuity. In 1914 Inoue Kaoru visited Ōkuma Shigenobu. The two fell into recollection of the days when they had worked together in the early Meiji ministry of finance. "We couldn't have done it without you," Inoue said in effect, and Ōkuma modestly answered that they had in fact done very well without him. But then they both caught themselves and remembered to say that without the august virtue of the Meiji Emperor it never could have been done at all.[13]

The Background and the Setting

It would not do to let our appreciation of the Meiji statesmen blind us to the advantages of the situation in which they worked. It is true that contemporary observers saw little future for Japan, emphasized its weakness, and exaggerated its instability. But the interest in modernization of the last decade and more has radically changed our picture of the nineteenth-century setting for the Meiji Restoration. It will suffice to simply remind ourselves of its features.

R. P. Dore's studies of education and literacy have shown that Japan was scarcely behind the Western world in her percentage of literate adults, and that a very large proportion of the population got some schooling outside the family. The importance of this for appropriation of other learning requirements in modern administration and industrialization, and the gain for unity through the government's ability to post its notices and have them read, to issue pamphlets and have them reach their target, must have been incalculable. The studies of political thought by Webb, Harootunian, and Earle have shown how Confucian scholarship assimilated the imperial tradition and blended with Shintō nationalism. Grant Goodman has traced the rise and spread of interest in the scientific learning of the West via the Dutch at Nagasaki, so that despite the centuries of seclusion there was a lively vogue for Western learning long before the coming of Perry. Thomas Smith showed how developments in agriculture transformed it from the extended family production of late medieval times into the modern small-holding village with its responsiveness to market advantages provided by the great Tokugawa cities. And Robert Bellah analyzed the codes of merchant values and practicality that accompanied this development in town and country. John Hall best describes the complexity of bureaucratic rationality that replaced the simple feudal controls of early Tokugawa times, and Albert Craig and I have tried to show how these currents came to focus in individual lives and particular domains in the crisis years of the 1860's. Nationalism was sufficiently pervasive, loyalty sufficiently unchallengeable, and economic and political problems sufficiently burdensome to make most feudal lords glad to surrender their authority in return for honor and reward when the Meiji government asked them to.

Perhaps most important of all was the sense of crisis that stirred the military elite as the centuries of seclusion were broken by the appearance of the West. Confrontation with new weapons, techniques, and enemies, opportunity to compete in appropriation of these possibilities, changed forever lives that had seemed stuck in the torpor of inherited rank and traditional authority. The discovery that their country was incapable of resisting the Western threat was decisive for a generation of samurai. It stirred them to individualism, idealism, resistance, terror, and finally reform, and out of it came a determination to avoid for their descendants the shame and fear that they had experienced.

The nineteenth-century Japanese thought themselves unlucky to be so pressed, and many foreign students have agreed. There is a large literature which explains the inadequacies of modern Japan's experiment with representative rule in terms of the short time-span in which it had to be compressed. But there needs to be more of a literature emphasizing the elements of good fortune. For it was probably a good deal easier to catch up in the nineteenth century than it has been in the twentieth century. Japan still had a modest population, and the death rate did not fall until industrialization had been begun. Antibiotics might have complicated the picture enormously. And Japan's speedy change, by contemporary needs, may even seem leisurely. Robert Ward points out that "in a number of important respects the amount of time required for the political modernization of Japan has not been much shorter than that required in the classic Western cases."[14] And Professor Katō, the sociologist I referred to earlier, groups Japan and America partly because, he suggests, their industrialization began at about the same time, after the civil strife of the nineteenth century.

Even the international climate could have been a good deal worse. The Western countries alarmed but they did not really threaten Japan. China and Korea could not help, but neither did they obstruct, and Japan's greater success quickly established her as the most likely recipient of outside help. Japan grew to power under the protection of the British fleet.

None of this would have sufficed of itself, and none of it lessens the achievement. But it should help to keep us from making easy transfers from the Japanese experiences to that of more recently developing societies. The lessons to be drawn are those of the importance of preparation, nationalism, of political stability, and steady motivation, rather than more specific items of comparison and application.

In Retrospect

There is another dimension of an event like the Meiji Restoration. It is what it has come to mean for the Japanese. And it is of relevance to note that while no historian can deny its paramount importance for Japan and indeed for the modern world, neither can he forget what sharply divided responses it has stirred within Japan.

It began in the 1860's. The quick coup that outmaneuvered the Tokugawa shogun and drove him into the position of rebel brought distrust and doubt from many parts of the country. Then, as the Meiji government grew in strength, its rivals—the leaders of the popular rights movement, and conservatives who disapproved of the degree of westernization—began to see it as a new kind of interest group, or shogunate, standing between emperor and people. The textbooks of the public education system unwittingly worked to reinforce some of these doubts. They taught that the emperor was virtuous and his people loyal, both by definition and instinct. The only thing that could go wrong therefore was the government, whose ministers sometimes pursued selfish ends and betrayed their trust. And since politics is necessarily imperfect, the thrust of the Confucian-moral teaching was one of disapproval for government, out of professed love for the emperor beyond it.

So it is striking to find that political radicals of all persuasions have claimed for themselves the mantle and purity of the Restoration activists. The anarchist Kōtoku Shūsui, executed in 1911 for alleged complicity in an attack on the emperor's life, styled himself a *shishi*—a man of high purpose—of the Restoration;[15] and the ultranationalist and military terrorists of the 1930's claimed that they, no less, were working for a Shōwa restoration that would complete the work left unfinished by their Meiji forebears. Thus Nishida Mitsugi wrote in 1922 that those who followed the Restoration leaders "did not understand the ideal and forgot the true principles. They severed the direct relations between the people and their sacrosanct, sublime and beloved Emperor, and put between them a barrier made of stupid, wicked, and unscrupulous men."[16] In present-day Japan one finds the struggling rightist organizations making determined efforts to capitalize on the historical effusion of the centennial and the remembered patriotism of the Meiji Restoration to prepare for another, or perhaps the same, Shōwa Restoration. Indeed, no one seems quite persuaded the Meiji Restoration finished its work. The Marxist historians who have long dominated the Japanese academies continue to write voluminously of the ways in which the Restoration stopped short of fundamental change, and often evoke a curious correspondence with their right-wing foes.

It would require a different, and longer, discussion to explore all the reasons for these views. One reason is certainly the association of morality with politics, a notion as old as Shintoism and one renewed by the Restoration claim for the unity of politics and worship. Total claims produce total discontent, and the failure of political overturn to produce solutions, at one blow, has frequently seemed conclusive for headstrong young men impatient with process and insistent on perfection.

In addition, of course, during the years since World War II there has developed a new and deeper sort of discontent with what the modern state achieved, and a determination that the injustice and the cost of militarist Japan shall not be forgotten in praise for the modernization that made it possible.

Out of this comes a setting in which the centennial celebration is, in the truest sense, controversial. It has awakened the decades-long argument between intellectuals and government, education ministry and teachers; it has stimulated both the right and left wings to a flurry of activity, fund-raising, and pronouncement. And, taken in conjunction with the time for renewal or reappraisal of Japan's security links with the United States in the 1970's, it has acquired a dramatic relevance for the historian who looks for links between his times and those that have gone before.

NOTES

1. Satsuma-Tosa argument quoted in Marius B. Jansen, *Sakamoto Ryōma and the Meiji Restoration* (Princeton, 1961), p. 300.
2. Katō Hidetoshi, "Kindaika to gendaika" (Modernity and contemporaneity), *Chūō Kōron* (Feb. 1968), pp. 66-85.
3. Quoted in F. V. Dickins and S. Lane-Poole, *The Life of Sir Harry Parkes* (London, 1894), II, 98.
4. Quoted by Maruyama Masao, "Kaikoku" (Opening the country), in *Koza: gendai rinri* (Symposium: contemporary ethics) Vol. II: *Tenkanki rinri shisō* (Ethical thought at periods of critical change; Tokyo, 1959), p. 98.
5. Hirao Michio, *Yamauchi Yōdō* (Tokyo, 1961), pp. 236 f.
6. Maruyama, "Kaikoku," p. 102, quoting *Dajōkan nisshi* (Council of state diary) No. 49.
7. Thomas C. Smith, "Japan's Aristocratic Revolution," *Yale Review*, Spring 1961.
8. See Roger F. Hackett, "Political Modernization and the Meiji Genrō," in R. E. Ward, ed., *Political Development in Modern Japan* (Princeton, 1968).
9. "Ishin no seishin to kōsō" (The spirit and concept of the restoration), *Tembō* (June 1968), p. 44.
10. Irokawa Daikichi, in *ibid.*, p. 42.
11. See, for example, R. K. Beardsley, J. W. Hall, and R. E. Ward, *Village Japan* (Chicago, 1959), pp. 354-55; and Robert E. Ward, "The Socio-Political Role of the *buraku* (hamlet) in Japan," *American Political Science Review*, LXV.4: 1030 f. (Dec. 1951).
12. See Tsuda Shigemayo, ed., Sasaki Takayuki, *Meiji Seijō to shin Takayuki* (The sacred Meiji emperor and his subject Takayuki; Tokyo, 1928), p. 730.
13. *Segai Inoue Kō den* (Biography of Inoue; Tokyo, 1933–34), 5:352.
14. Ward, ed., *Political Development in Modern Japan*, p. 589.
15. F. G. Notehelfer, "Kōtoku Shūsui: Portrait of a Japanese Radical" (unpublished Ph.D. dissertation, Princeton University, 1968).
16. From *Mugen shiron* (Shallow and private view), reprinted in Hashikawa Bunzō, ed., *Chōkokka shugi* (Ultranationalism), Vol. 31: *Gendai Nihon shisō taikei* (Outline of contemporary Japanese thought; Tokyo, 1964), p. 72. I owe this reference to Mr. Ben-Ami Shillony.

Political Assassination in Early Meiji Japan: The Plot Against Ōkubo Toshimichi

Sidney DeVere Brown
University of Illinois (Visiting 1968-1969)

Now that evidence of the success of Meiji Japan's experiment in modernization is abundant, it is customary to insert indices of economic growth and other proof of progress in papers on that era. But Japan's modernization had another side. It had a dark underside where social tensions erupted periodically in violence. Balanced consideration of the period, therefore, requires attention to the aims and frustrations of men left out of society as well as to the purposes of the ruling elite. It requires study of the patterns of violence which emerged when those disinherited by the reforms of the era rallied to the standard of rebel leader or took up the assassin's sword.[1]

Some assassinations are random acts by psychopathic individuals; others are carefully conceived plots based on the grievances of large social groups. The political murder under study here, the bloody attack on Home Minister Ōkubo Toshimichi on the morning of May 14, 1878, was the latter type. It was a confrontation by samurai traditionalists, who felt wronged by policies which destroyed their hereditary class privileges, with the minister who dominated the modernizing cabinet.[2] Ōkubo's charisma was the charisma of change, and this instance of violence against change provides a microcosm of broader social and political clashes of the period.

Some assassins strike from the shadows and melt into the multitude to conceal their crimes; others commit political murder with a view to maximum publicity and martyrdom. Ōkubo's killers, who surrendered at once, having given their apologia—their *zankanjō*—to the press, belonged to the second class, the righteous lawbreakers. They aimed to "carry benevolence beyond the grave" and through their own deaths by execution to win widespread sympathy for their cause. In some measure they succeeded.

Ōkubo, like Lincoln, was murdered in the aftermath of victory by the central government in civil war. Unlike the American, Ōkubo did not become the martyred man of sorrows. Rather, his assassins won popular adulation. The real interest of the assassination, therefore, centers on the public sympathy given the attackers. This exposition, in addition to bringing together the threads of the assassination plot, will touch on the romantic tradition of the assassin as folk hero in Japan.

Let us consider now the attack of May 14, 1878, the motivations of the attackers, their rationale, and some responses to the attack.

The Attack: May 14, 1878

The state business that preoccupied Ōkubo as he called his carriage to leave for the palace on the morning of May 14, 1878, was portentous. The matters that concerned him were internal security, economic development, and greater centralization of political authority—the very issues which inflamed the six assassins who lay in wait along his route.

The return of domestic order was scheduled for celebration in the council of state[3] meeting before the throne that morning with presentation of awards to army and navy heroes of the successful struggle against the counterrevolutionary forces of Saigō Takamori in the southwest the previous year. As councillor, Ōkubo was to be present when the Emperor Meiji elevated General Torio Koyata, for example, to the senior second court rank and conferred on him an annual pension of 600 yen.[4]

But a chance caller turned Ōkubo's mind to the national economic development program—even as his carriage driver waited at the front entrance. Governor Yamayoshi Morisuke of Fukushima prefecture, in Tokyo for the recent meeting of the assembly of local officials, came for final instructions from his administrative superior before leaving for the northeast. As the home minister completed dressing in his parlor, he conferred with the apologetic governor. Ordinarily taciturn, Ōkubo was now eloquent and optimistic as he outlined his plans to force the pace of economic modernization. Limited progress in the revolt-plagued decade since the Meiji Restoration marked but a beginning, he said. During the second decade, just ahead, when "we shall put internal administration in good order and make national power a reality," he expected to direct an economic development program of unprecedented dimensions. Ōkubo admonished Yamayoshi to supervise the new Asaka land reclamation project in Fukushima with greatest care, for this effort to drain the upland swamps of the northeast was a model of its kind—a prototype for many similar projects that would expand the cultivated acreage and provide a livelihood for some of the declassed samurai. In his meeting with the prefectural governors at the Hama detached palace the previous day Ōkubo had observed that some displayed a notable skepticism about the 12,500,000 yen industrial bond program under which such local development projects were to be financed; and Ōkubo charged his departing visitor with responsibility for the success of this model effort.[5]

A desire to purge the rolls of laggard governors possibly lay behind the hasty note which Ōkubo dispatched to Itō Hirobumi that morning by messenger. Perhaps Ōkubo urged Councillor Itō to attend the morning's meeting to lend support on this personnel matter; for the home minister shared with the council of state the appointment and removal power over governors, some of whom, apart from lassitude, seemed politically unreliable. Itō, as president of the recent assembly of local officials, had encountered a direct challenge from these appointees; and he might be expected to lend strong support to his patron in eliminating these discordant voices. Ōkubo's critics assert that he was preparing this additional step toward political absolutism as he left for the palace.[6] The time was 8:10 A.M.[7]

The minister who rode in his English-style two-horse closed carriage was "the least distinctively Japanese" among the members of the ruling oligarchy and had "a strong dash of the European."[8] The home that he left behind was an expensive, two-story, painted, Western-style mansion, one of the first in Tokyo; and the sight outraged traditionalists.[9] Dressed in morning coat and trousers with cravat and high collar, Ōkubo, with sidewhiskers and mustache aping the style favored by Occidental statesmen he had met abroad in 1873, had the appearance of the elegant European gentleman. His coachman took the usual route from the house near the present National Diet Building in Kasumigaseki to the temporary Akasaka palace, some distance west of the main palace, which had burned nine days earlier.

The six conspirators who waited ahead at a deserted spot along the road in Kioi-chō were dressed in a contrasting traditional manner that highlighted their quarrel with Ōkubo.[10] All carried swords, once the badge of samurai rank, but outlawed by imperial edict in 1876. The ringleader, Shimada Ichirō (1848-1878), who had gathered the conspirators at his Yotsuya lodgings at dawn to proceed to this lonely stretch of road, wore a padded black kimono of finest *habutae* silk with family crest. Most of the others wore the *hakama* divided-skirt, but tied their loose *uwagi* coats about their waists to allow freedom of arm movement. They presented (except for one incongruous derby hat) a picture of old-fashioned Japanese samurai gathering for a vendetta.

As they awaited the carriage they knew by sight, the two lookouts along the road, Shimada and Chō Rengō (1856-1878), played with flowering peony branches, a flower never afterwards used by the Ōkubo family. The conspirators' meticulous investigation had revealed that the vehicle would appear at this exact time and place, for the councillors always gathered at the palace on days ending in four and nine and Ōkubo's coachman invariably took this route.[11] Beyond a low earthen wall on the left-hand side of the road, concealed by an outbuilding amidst rank grass and mulberry trees on the property of the court noble Mibu Tomonaga, crouched their four confederates. The ashen-gray cloudy sky which threatened rain provided an ominous setting.

When the groom who stood on the platform at the rear of Ōkubo's carriage caught sight of the two loiterers, he dropped off to run ahead for a closer look.[12] A sword blow that barely grazed his hat let the groom know that he had encountered danger, so he sprinted through the ambush to call for help at the estate of Prince Kitashirakawa on the right. The time for help was past, however, for the carriage had already reached the ambush. Just as the coachman whipped his horses to make the sharp left turn that began the long steep climb up Kioi-zaka to the palace, Chō Rengō struck the foreleg of the horse on the right with his long sword. The glancing blow merely caused the horse to neigh loudly and surge forward. But the next blow, a clean one, delivered by Sugimoto Otogiku (1849-1878) who jumped over the low fence to join the attack, nearly severed the other horse's foreleg and halted the vehicle.

When coachman Nakamura Tarō leaped from the driver's box shouting and flailing his whip, Wakita Kōichi (1850-1878) dispatched the unfortunate man with a single deep cut across the left shoulder and chest. At the same time, Ōkubo, who had been studying documents intently, looked up to find his carriage surrounded by conspirators who had swarmed out of the unkempt Mibu property, joined now by their leaders. "Wait!" he called, "Do you have some request to make?" "What! At this stage!" one responded. The home minister impassively wrapped his papers in a woolen *furoshiki,* after which he tried to escape from the carriage, or possibly was pulled. But at his first step down, Shimada's sword blow from above opened a wound from midforehead to eyebrow. As Ōkubo fell, blows rained on the back of his head, his spine, and his legs. A short sword thrust deeply into the side of his neck stayed fixed when the conspirators took hasty flight. Ōkubo, mortally wounded, rose twice to drag himself short distances across the dew-drenched grass before he collapsed for the last time, face up.

While the groom ran to the Akasaka-mitsuke police station to give the alarm, the six assassins hurried across the Mibu property to turn themselves in to the guard at the palace gate. There the commanding Shimada announced in a bold voice, "We have just now waylaid Ōkubo Toshimichi in Kioi-chō, while he was on his way to the cabinet meeting, and assassinated him. We have disposed of him properly and our purpose is done." In confirmation two companions wore blood-stained *hakama*. To an official of the imperial household ministry, Shimada handed their apologia, a strange dualistic statement of purpose, in which the conspirators proclaimed themselves both as avengers of Saigō Takamori, who died in defense of Japanese tradition, and as reformers calling for European parliamentarianism. Their faces were wreathed in smiles as they awaited the arrival of police officers for the arrest.[13]

Formation of the Conspiracy

The man who brought Ōkubo to his death was Shimada Ichirō, *shizoku* of Ishikawa prefecture. "I conceived the idea of the assassination," confessed Shimada; and all evidence corroborates that his was no idle boast. Years of teahouse gossip jelled into a definite plot to strike down Ōkubo to aid the Saigō rebellion in April 1877. The plot, conceived in support of the Saigō uprising, became, as the march of events outdated it, a substitute for rebellion to check "mistaken" government policies. With rare singleness of purpose Shimada and his principal accomplice,

Chō Rengō, worked for more than a year to perfect their conspiracy, recruiting along the way several loyal disciples. By April 1878, Shimada's obsession had become an open secret in Ishikawa —so much so that the prefectural governor wired a warning to the chief of the metropolitan police in Tokyo to maintain surveillance over the dangerous man who had headed for the capital. What then were the sources of Shimada's blinding hatred of Ōkubo?

A sense of personal failure must have been the starting point for Shimada's venture in assassination. He attributed to the oligarchy in Tokyo his inability to achieve prominence in the military services. Shimada's promising military career flourished during the war of the Meiji Restoration in 1868 when he fought with the Kaga-*han* army during its triumphant march through northern Echigo province on behalf of the imperial cause. This was the high point of his life, and battlefield promotions allowed him to advance his hereditary status of *ashigaru,* the lowest samurai class of foot-soldiers. By 1871, Shimada was a temporary first lieutenant in the reorganized *han* army. However, his ambitions were shattered by the abrupt dissolution of the Kaga-*han* army at the time of the abolition of fiefs and the creation of the first national military force. Failure seemed final after his brief unsuccessful effort to study Western military science at private schools in Osaka and Tokyo in 1872.

Career frustration brought to the surface a psychopathic personality which seemed to account for Shimada's predilection for the more radical side of every issue in *han* politics. He joined the righteous faction *(Seigi-ha)* of lower samurai rebels against the villainous faction *(Kambutsu-ha)* of higher fief families in 1871; and in 1875 he led an ultraradical group of samurai protestors committed to "direct action" to restore lost samurai rights.[14] Moderate, mainstream leaders of samurai protest were a bit wary of this husky samurai of "tempestuous temperament," who was forever sending angry letters to leaders of rival factions and engaging in feuds of obscure origin.

Kaga sectional spirit provided a milieu that reinforced personal tendencies and stirred intense hostility toward the Satsuma-Chōshū oligarchy in Tokyo. Hardly a Kaga man gained membership in the new national bureaucracy, and it outraged Shimada that neither he nor any Kaga soldier obtained a commission in the new national army in these years. In 1874 several hundred politically minded Kaga *shizoku* formed the Chūkokusha (Admonition Society) to restore the greatness that was Kaga's in the Tokugawa period when it had ranked first among *han* with a rated rice production of 1,027,000 *koku* and Lord Maeda had enjoyed a position of profound respect at Edo castle. The Chūkokusha was not a conspiratorial organization at first. It called primarily for a Kaga share in government through creation of a representative assembly. It charged that the Ōkubo-dominated oligarchy had forgotten the Meiji Emperor's promise in the Five Article Oath of 1868 to create "assemblies broadly convoked" and, thus, not freeze out any section. The Chūkokusha sent two delegates to Osaka in February 1875 for the first great national convention of liberal forces that organized the Aikokusha (Patriots' Society) under the leadership of Itagaki Taisuke. One of these delegates was Kuga Yoshinao, who later composed Shimada's assassination apologia, but Kuga was in 1875 part of the Chūkokusha mainstream leadership that regarded Shimada as a "rustic" and as too radical and erratic with his talk of physical force and direct action to be effective. Indeed, these leaders ejected Shimada and his numerous disciples from formal installation ceremonies for Chūkokusha members later that spring.[15] Still, Shimada breathed deeply of the spirit of Kaga sectionalism as preached by the Chūkokusha.

Loss of status as samurai added to the social strain which drove the Shimada group along its violent course.[16] His conspiracy was obviously the last bitter defiance of an anachronistic hereditary military class whose social and economic underpinnings had given way. Shimada rarely mentioned anything so crass, in samurai eyes, as money—or resentment over the loss he suffered with forced conversion of stipends to bonds; but he and his family lived a hand-to-mouth existence after 1876, saved only by the charity of a former high *han* official. Moreover, loss of status symbols figured as prominently as economic factors in stirring discontent. It was outlawry of sword-wearing that particularly angered Shimada, and he regularly defied this order from the central government.

These elements of social strain expressed themselves in violence partly because Japanese society accorded a measure of legitimacy to this kind of protest. Through the era of Tokugawa despotism, there developed a long romantic tradition of the assassin as folk hero who challenged an oppressive policy and, in his martyrdom, brought alteration of it.[17] More recently, the tradition had been reinvigorated by a series of assassinations that began with the killing of Great Elder Ii Naosuke in 1860. Ironically, Itō and perhaps others now in the oligarchy had molded in the 1860's the pattern which inspired Shimada; but they had already seen it turned against their colleagues earlier in the post-Restoration era when three major modernizers died at the hands of traditionalists: in 1869 Councillor Yokoi Shōnan, who expressed interest in democracy and Christianity; later the same year Vice Minister of War Ōmura Masujirō, who Europeanized the armed forces; and in 1871 Councillor Hirozawa Maomi, whose centralization policies angered his former Chōshū clansmen. The incidence of assassination rose with response to a pattern as one political murder suggested another. Ōkubo's killers were steeped in traditions of these earlier "martyred patriots" whose actions, therefore, triggered the 1878 affair.[18]

Another contributing element was the complete politicization of *shizoku* society in Ishikawa prefecture. *Han* schools of late Tokugawa created a "passionate concern with politics" among samurai, as R. P. Dore has demonstrated, and instilled in them civic responsibility for the fate of the nation. Beyond that, students read the romanticized histories which glorified the military exploits of the early feudal age and popularized the cult of the sword. Finally, they absorbed the Confucian doctrine that duty to principle superseded the duty of personal loyalty to a superior who might need to encounter defiance for his own good. This amalgam encouraged private individuals to resort to violence, particularly in the absence of alternative means of protest. The unusually high level of literacy in Ishikawa (85 percent literacy among conscripts from that prefecture in 1887) only intensified the degree of political involvement.[19] With the breakdown of older social and political controls immediately after the Restoration, before the authority of the home ministry really penetrated into the prefectures, such political activity sometimes burgeoned out of control. Indeed, minor police officials who were nominally home ministry officials were among Shimada's staunchest supporters.

Within this context the Ishikawa conspirators came together, angry men, involved politically and on the lookout for a cause that would support strong opposition to the Meiji leaders. Each man had his favorite cause. Chō Rengō responded to Saigō's plea to rebuild national power by reviving the pure untarnished samurai spirit in the private schools, and the young Ishikawa disciple returned from his two visits to Kagoshima imitating Saigō's simple pleasures as he took two hunting dogs into the mountains near the Ishikawa castle-town of Kanazawa to seek fox and badger. The unproved allegation that Home Minister Ōkubo sent an undercover agent into Satsuma to assassinate Saigō was the precipitating incident that moved Chō to plot with Shimada. By contrast, Wakita Kōichi was attracted to the representative assembly issue, and the summary rejection of his petition on behalf of an elective parliament by the prefectural office led him to resign his position as a middle-school teacher, ultimately to join the conspiracy. Shimada had still another ideological grievance. A howling expansionist, he regarded Ōkubo's moderate course in opposing invasion of Korea in 1873 and in arranging prompt evacuation of Taiwan in 1874 as an unpardonable weakness in foreign policy.[20] All three men were preoccupied with politics and fixed upon Ōkubo as the thwarter of their divergent causes.

That Shimada should emerge as the ringleader of the group plotting against Ōkubo was something of a curiosity. He belonged to the lowest stratum of samurai. At least three of his followers were from upper samurai families: of the 200 *koku* level (Chō and Sugimura) or of the 300 *koku* level (Wakita). Shimada was barely literate—a man who wrote his ideographs in a childish scrawl, while Chō was regarded as brilliant—"a jewel of a youth"[21]—and Wakita taught school. Apparently Shimada gloried in post-Restoration Ishikawa's freer atmosphere that allowed him to mingle with men of good family. They in turn were captivated by the charismatic, slightly older man with his jet-black, bristling beard and penetrating eyes. He was cut in the *shishi* pattern.

In the autumn of 1877 the plot thickened as Wakita went to Tokyo in advance of the rest, ostensibly to enroll in the new government Technical Institute *(Kangyō Gijuku)*. In a few weeks Chō Rengō, a sort of associate director of the assassination enterprise, followed Wakita to the capital to scout the situation. The sensitive Chō, his solemn, thin face ornamented by a tiny mustache, was the brains of the group; and in several letters he analyzed the problem for Shimada back in Kanazawa. The Tokyo force was augmented in December 1877 with the arrival of Chō's personal disciple, Sugimura Bun'ichi, to enroll in the same Technical Institute as Wakita. Sugimura was very young, notwithstanding his premature baldness, and this fact may explain his role as a shadowy figure, a follower not a leader. His submissive character was akin to that of Shimada's lackey, Sugimoto Otogiku, who reached Tokyo in April 1878. Sugimoto was an odd, dwarfish man, nicknamed "The Buddha" because of his curly hair. The only non-Ishikawa conspirator was Asai Hisaatsu (1853-1878), a former policeman from Shimane prefecture. Asai literally forced his way into the plot. As a policeman on duty in Tokyo he had been mobilized to fight against the Satsuma rebels in 1877 and decorated for bravery, but he spent much of his two-week leave granted as a reward in a house of prostitution. For this breach of regulations he was dismissed from the police force with the approval of the home minister. Asai joined, therefore, for the narrowest kind of personal revenge. Meantime, his band assembled, Shimada left Kanazawa on March 25, 1878, paused to pray at the shrine of imperial loyalist Kusunoki Masashige near Kobe, and reached Chō's lodgings in Tokyo on April 7 or 8.[22]

It was Shimada who commanded the band that appeared at the palace gate on May 14. In his confession Shimada explained, "We surrendered to the guard at the palace because we had recorded our principal objectives in doing this deed in our Assassination Apologia which we carried. We wished to hand this over (to His Majesty, the Emperor)."[23]

Assassination Rationale

The apologia which the six handed over was in fact addressed to the masses as much as to the emperor. This became evident as Shimada played out his role melodramatically before an official of the imperial household ministry. Aware that the difficulty of the ideographs and the elegance of the calligraphy did not tally with the rustic manner of Shimada, the official asked, "Who is involved in this besides you?" The assassin avoided answering directly that the Ishikawa journalist Kuga Yoshinao had composed the statement for Shimada. Rather, he proclaimed grandly, "Our thirty million people—all are our allies as we eliminate the tyrannical officials." To make doubly sure that the document came to the attention of the people, Shimada arranged for a confederate to leave copies of it at the offices of two newspapers at the hour of the assassination. One of them, the *Chōya Shimbun,* a Tokyo daily, published extracts from it.[24]

The main thrust of the argument in this document was that laws of the time were derived neither from the emperor's will nor from the people, but were the arbitrary creations of a few self-appointed leaders. Elimination of these men who had come between the emperor and his people was justified, the statement continued, now that the fear of Saigō no longer kept corruption within bounds. But those who deserved to die were so many and the conspirators so few that the six could not dispatch all of the "evil officials." They selected Ōkubo as the chief symbol of mistaken government policy, believing that his murder would overawe the rest and somehow restore a desirable state of affairs.[25]

Their strategy of revolution consisted almost entirely of a few powerful phrases. "If the root and trunk be eliminated, the branches and leaves will wither away." Changing imagery, the rationale evoked an apocalyptic vision of a single dramatic act that would "stir the public spirit in all corners of the land, and restore the fallen fortunes of the nation." This revolutionary strategy did not embrace planning beyond the assassination plot. Its instigators assumed that, thenceforth, things were automatically going to happen to bring an imperial restoration, popular government, or some other desirable end.

A strange mixture of traditionalist and modern objectives ran through the apologia. In the list of charges against Ōkubo, the assassins condemned him, on the one hand, for economic modernization policies which ruined the samurai class, but on the other they denounced him just as vehemently for delay in political modernization which would have allowed representative institutions to vent their grievances.

The language of the five formal charges preferred against Ōkubo has a force and directness which makes quotation worthwhile. Ōkubo's first crime was that he had blocked the move for representative government, contrary to the promise given in the Five Article Oath and made more definite in 1875. To quote the exact words, "He has ignored public opinion, suppressed the people's rights, and, thereby, seized absolute power for himself." So-called crimes two and three related to Ōkubo's use of tax money for corrupt or frivolous purposes. "His second crime: he has conducted the administration for private ends, openly countenanced corruption, and extended his influence and fortune as he pleased. His third crime: he has carried out low priority construction projects, put up useless buildings which are mere ornaments, and, thereby, exhausted the nation's finances." Corruption, in the minds of the conspirators, had made the government into a kind of a merchant house from which officials started their own companies or exerted public influence for private ends—Inoue Kaoru's manipulations in copper mining, for example. Lavish expenditures drew censure as Ōkubo put up expensive public buildings, furnished the palace luxuriously, installed gaslights in Tokyo, and spread railways and telegraph lines through the land. The vigor and bustle of Europe during his visit in 1873 has deluded him into believing that these visible ornaments created national strength. The fourth crime was the reverse face of the spendthrift policy: "He has alienated patriotic samurai, causing rebellions." Not only had samurai stipends stopped; in Shimada's inverted world, the government had precipitated the Saga rebellion of 1874 by striking against a minor samurai protest meeting. Next, in 1877 the government tried to assassinate the Great Saigō, and—when he started his march on Tokyo—declared him a criminal and rebel without a hearing. Ōkubo's fifth and final crime derived from all the others. "He has blundered in foreign policy and lost the national rights." The expansionist-minded Ishikawa assassin had in mind "humiliations" to Japan in Korea, Karafuto, the Ryukyu Islands, and elsewhere.[26]

This apologia represented Shimada's effort to use the imperial institution, the central myth of the state, to promote his own cause. He identified his political dissidence with imperial loyalism, and touched a responsive chord in the nation.[27] Ōkubo, the subject who was guilty of "subordination of the imperial line," was also responsible for "impoverishment of the masses." Ōkubo's elimination, therefore, would effect imperial restoration and end samurai poverty, Shimada reasoned.

Shimada also invoked the *shishi* tradition of the brave and loyal defender of principle, who goes to death defiant and unrepentant, thus proving his sincerity. In his last exhortation to his eight-year-old son, Shimada explained that "loyalty to principle *(meibun taigi)* bears little relationship to victory or defeat." Often the righteous fail—Saigō for example; whereas traitors to the imperial house succeed—Hōjō Yoshitoki (who crushed Emperor Go-Toba in 1221) and Ashikaga Takauji (who deserted the cause of Emperor Go-Daigo in 1336), both sinister prototypes of Ōkubo. Had Shimada been successful, like the United States revolutionaries against England, he would no longer be considered a rebel but a hero, he told his son in a farewell evocative of both his limited vision and his sense of righteousness.[28]

Responses to the Assassination

On July 27, 1878, Shimada and his band received the capital punishment that they expected and invited by confessing before the justice ministry's special court established to try them. Judge Tamano Seiri sentenced them to death at 10 A.M., and executioners beheaded the six in the yard of Ichigaya prison in Tokyo at 11:30 A.M. the same day. Shimada played out his role as *shishi* to the end, encouraging his comrades to die bravely and leading the way without flinching. He requested only that his bonds be loosened. Asked if he had last words, he merely said, "Nothing."[29]

As the men had anticipated, Ishikawa prefecture virtually canonized them for their deed and their deaths. Ishikawa men reclaimed their remains, and in 1879 buried them with honor in a scenic spot beneath the pines at the foot of Mount Noda on the outskirts of their old castle-town of Kanazawa. In time, the myth of the heroic assassins received the official imprimatur as it appeared in the prefectural history, hardly diluted. This official publication devoted more than a hundred pages to the conspiracy, providing a long, sympathetic account that turned it into an epic. It may not be coincidental that Kuga Yoshinao (1843-1916), author of the apologia, on his release from life imprisonment in the Emperor Meiji's general amnesty of 1889, became archivist and historian for the house of his old feudal lord.[30]

The nation as a whole was less enthusiastic than Ishikawa, but not altogether condemnatory. Those who mourned Ōkubo were chiefly his acquaintances. Even in Tokyo there was glorification of the assassins, as in Yoshikawa's 1879 biographical novel on Shimada. The author portrayed the assassin as a sentimental patriot and stirred sympathy for the brotherhood of conspirators by relating their Robin Hood exploits. To be sure, some newspapers condemned the action forthrightly, mostly government papers such as the *Nichi Nichi Shimbun*. Opposition papers said little in the face of tight government control under the Press Law of 1875; for the *Chōya Shimbun* received a ten-day suspension for publishing part of the assassination apologia, an action "injurious to the peace of the country." The flourishing foreign-language press, whose editors were shielded by extraterritoriality, had freedom to say what opposition Japanese editors only felt. Typical was the *Japan Daily Herald,* which scored the "morbid and perverted feeling of patriotism" that provoked the violence but expressed grudging praise for men whose act was "redeemed by unselfish sacrifice." The *Herald* then identified the source of the plot with the "faulty method of government" that brought "despotic suppression of expression of opinion through the press—the safety valve of nations" and "denial of representative government."[31]

In what degree did such veiled sympathy move government policy toward the assassins' stated aims—toward representative government, less state support for economic enterprise, and a strong foreign policy? Immediate policy changes were imperceptible, except for assignment of police guards for cabinet ministers. Shortly afterwards, perhaps there was some official response in the edict of July 22, 1878, implementing the earlier proposal of the assembly of local officials for election of legislatures in both urban and rural prefectures. Moreover, reduction of government support for economic modernization commenced about this time and culminated in the sale of many government enterprises in 1881. Professor Tsuchiya Takao regards the assassination as one factor, a subordinate one, in the policy change. No immediate foreign-policy shift resulted; but the long-range significance of the assassination lay in the fact that the conspirators of 1878 revived and popularized a behavioral pattern that twentieth-century members of the radical right used to move the nation toward war, expansion, and defeat.

NOTES

1. American studies of social change "tend to lack the elements of violence, revolution, class, and ideology," concerned as they are with "continuities and the role of tradition in stabilizing social change." For this bias Japanese scholars frequently criticize American writings on their nation's history. John Whitney Hall, "Reflections on a Centennial," *Journal of Asian Studies,* XXVII, 4:718 (August 1968).

2. All six participants in the attack on Ōkubo were *shizoku,* a class that included a substantial portion of the old samurai retainers. One of them signed the group's apologia as a commoner, or *heimin;* but, in fact, Wakita Kōichi sprang from an important 300-*koku* samurai family. He had only recently removed his name from the family register to protect his relatives from the consequences of the plot. Hioki Ken, ed., *Ishikawa-ken shi* (History of Ishikawa prefecture), 5 vols. (Tokyo, 1939–40), IV, 1159.

3. Ōkubo held the position of councillor, or *sangi,* in addition to his ad-

ministrative post as home minister. The council of state, a policy-making body, met at the palace six times monthly.

4. Tokyo *Nichi Nichi Shimbun,* May 15, 1878, in Nakayama Yasumasa, ed., *Shimbun shūsei Meiji hennen shi* (Documentary history of the Meiji era in newspapers), 15 vols. (Tokyo, 1934–36), III, 390; *Japan Weekly Mail,* May 18, 1878.

5. Katsuda Magoya, *Ōkubo Toshimichi den* (Biography of Ōkubo Toshimichi), 3 vols. (Tokyo, 1910–11), III, 769–70.

6. Discussions at Itō's house that morning between Itō and Takasaki Seifū, Ōkubo's close associate, plus Sasaki Takayuki had centered on the possibility that Ōkubo might take charge of the chamberlains of the palace while Itō moved up to home minister. *Ibid.,* III, 770–74.

7. There is a family tradition that the departure was delayed slightly by the cries of Ōkubo's two-year-old daughter, whom the father normally carried to the *genkan* before handing her back to her mother, but on this occasion only the baby refused to leave her father. To quiet her crying Ōkubo took the girl into the carriage for a ride around the circular drive before handing her out at the back door. Interview with Mrs. Ijūin (the daughter) by author, Tokyo, August 23, 1957.

8. Editorial, *Japan Daily Herald,* May 22, 1878.

9. Cricket grounds were even laid out on the lawn. This structure had created controversy from the start, and legend has it that Saigō in Kagoshima allegedly decided on the final break with his boyhood friend Ōkubo in 1877 on seeing a photograph of the costly home.

10. Ironically the mansion of the Great Elder Ii Naosuke, victim of the spectacular assassination plot of 1860, stood near this spot. The very name of the place, Kioi, was derived from the names of the daimyo whose estates were located there in the Tokugawa era: the lord of Kii, the lord of Owari, and the Ii family.

11. *Ishikawa-ken shi,* IV, 1124.

12. Ōkubo was virtually unguarded despite one earlier serious attempt on his life and numerous threats. Futaki Chūsaku, Kagoshima *shizoku,* had been sentenced to prison for the 1876 assassination attempt. On the minimal plans for Ōkubo's protection see the 1929 interview with the groom Odaka Yoshikichi (who was then eighty) by Ishiguro Tadamori as published in Murobuse Tetsurō, *Nihon no terorisuto* (Japanese terrorists; Tokyo, 1962), pp. 85–86.

13. Ironically, it was Councillor Saigō Tsugumichi, younger brother of the Great Saigō, who hurried to his fallen colleague Ōkubo and accompanied the remains back to the Ōkubo mansion.

This account of the assassination is based on the following primary and secondary sources: Murobuse Tetsurō, *Nihon no terorisuto,* pp. 83–88; *Ishikawa-ken shi,* IV, 1124–30; Katsuda, *Ōkubo Toshimichi den,* III, 768–74; Tokyo *Nichi Nichi Shimbun,* May 15, 1878, in *Meiji hennen shi,* III, 389–90; *Japan Daily Herald,* May 15, 1878; Tanaka Sōgorō, *Ōkubo Toshimichi* (Tokyo, 1938), pp. 440–44.

14. Members of the righteous faction maintained close ties with Satsuma, which displayed traditionalist and separatist tendencies; the villainous faction sided with the central government, which was committed to policies of modernization and political unification.

15. Sugimura Bun'ichi (1860–78), younger brother of Chūkokusha chief Sugimura Kansei, joined the assassination conspiracy of 1878.

16. Reference is made on this and the following pages to Neil J. Smelser, *Theory of Collective Behavior* (New York, 1962), *passim*.

17. The incidence of assassination in the Tokugawa period was not great by modern Japanese standards, but a few celebrated deeds of violence gained wide public approval. In 1684 the "able but arbitrary" Great Elder Hotta Masatoshi had been killed by one of the junior elders. Edwin O. Reischauer and John K. Fairbank, *East Asia: the Great Tradition* (Boston, 1960), p. 620. More sensational was the assassination of the Junior Elder Tanuma Mototomo by an infuriated palace guardsman who believed that his own genealogy was being used by the parvenu Tanuma to forge his aristocratic credentials. Hereditary aristocrats all approved; moreover, conservative forces generally welcomed this as a censure of Tanuma's father, innovationist head of government. John W. Hall, *Tanuma Okitsugu 1719–1788: Forerunner of Modern Japan* (Cambridge, 1955), p. 39, pp. 42–43.

18. Information about Shimada comes primarily from *Ishikawa-ken shi*, IV, 240–82. For a revealing account of the motivation of Tsuge Shirōzaemon in assassinating Yokoi Shōnan see Mori Ōgai, *Ōgai zenshū* (Complete works of Ōgai; Tokyo, 1936), VI, 36–74. Professor David Abosch of Northern Illinois University called my attention to the latter.

19. R. P. Dore, "The Legacy of Tokugawa Education," in Marius B. Jansen, ed., *Changing Japanese Attitudes toward Modernization* (Princeton, 1965), pp. 100 fn., 117–19.

20. Shimada had met Saigō at the time the Satsuma leader was prominent as advocate of an attack on Korea, and Shimada was charmed by the great man. Even when overseas expansion took place, however, Shimada was denied glory; for, though he volunteered for the Taiwan expedition in 1874, he was not invited to join.

21. Judge Tamano Seiri, who conducted the trial of the conspirators, was reputed to have given this praise. *Ishikawa-ken shi*, IV, 1157–58.

22. *Ishikawa-ken shi*, IV, 1156–62.

23. Shimada's Confession, signed July 6, 1878, reprinted in Katsuda, *Ōkubo Toshimichi den*, III, 779–83.

24. *Chōya Shimbun*, May 15, 1878; *Ishikawa-ken shi*, IV, 1125.

25. In the apologia the conspirators asserted, "Kido Takayoshi, Ōkubo Toshimichi, and Iwakura Tomomi—these were the ringleaders. Nor could we tolerate Ōkuma Shigenobu, Itō Hirobumi, Kuroda Kiyotaka, or Kawaji Toshiyoshi. In addition, if we consider Sanjō Sanetomi and corruptionists of his stripe, the number of small-time hangers-on is countless." Kido had received consideration as the target of the assassins. "Unexpectedly Takayoshi died of illness. This must have been the will of Heaven, that one of the great corruptionists should come to his end thus." Apologia text in Katsuda, *Ōkubo Toshimichi den*, III, 777–78.

26. Ōkubo's effective personal negotiations in Peking in 1874 received short shrift in Ishikawa on the grounds that the government tried to pass off China's payment for roads and repairs in Taiwan as an indemnity. For text and supplementary explanation of the apologia see *Ishikawa-ken shi*, IV, 1125-43; Katsuda, *Ōkubo Toshimichi den*, III, 776–80.

27. The rationale for this is traced in Herschel Webb, *The Japanese Imperial Institution in the Tokugawa Period* (New York, 1968), 247–59.
28. Text of the farewell message in *Ishikawa-ken shi,* IV, 1152–55.
29. *Ibid.,* IV, 1145–49. Seventeen other Ishikawa men received sentences ranging from life to one hundred days for involvement. In addition, a luckless Tokyo policeman from Ishikawa wrote his brother in Kanazawa in praise of the assassins' "glorious deed," for which expression of sentiment he received thirty days.
30. Before the assassination, on May 9, 1878, Kuga fled Tokyo; and he was employed as editor of the *Ise Shimbun* when he was arrested on May 22 at a public bath in the city of Ise. Employees of the paper subsequently gave a banquet in his honor. *Ishikawa-ken shi,* IV, 1162.
31. Editorial, *Japan Daily Herald,* May 17, 1878. Ōkubo was given the first state funeral in modern times, and thousands participated in the procession to Aoyama cemetery, where his remains were interred. Behind his tomb were buried the coachman and the horse who had been in the home minister's service. On the horse's stone marker is an image of the faithful beast as if for a T'ang emperor.

The Otsu Affair:
The Formation of Japan's Judicial Conscience

Barbara Teters
Iowa State University

As the goal of modernization preceded that of democratization by some three-quarters of a century, so did the establishment of rule-by-law in the Meiji era precede the fulfillment of the rule-of-law after World War II. Seventy-seven years separated 1945, and its promise of the rule-of-law, from 1868 and the Charter Oath. During that time, the principle of rule-by-law—that is, government by statute, ordinance, and regulation—replaced the Tokugawa system, which Henderson has called the rule-by-status; rule-by-law was adopted and applied with remarkable vigor and consistency by generations of men who did not yet accept the proposition that the law itself must be subject to a higher law.[1] Nonetheless, early in the modern period the fragile presence of the rule-of-law became apparent in the form of judicial independence. As a result of the Otsu crisis in which that principle was tested and established, the atmosphere in which the individual daily confronted his government and the presuppositions on both sides regarding that confrontation were basically, although ever so slightly, altered in the direction of the supremacy of law. Japan thus took a small but significant step toward constitutionalism.

Article 57 of the Meiji constitution consisted of an explicit statement of the principle of judicial independence. The meaning and durability of that constitutional provision were challenged two years after the constitution was promulgated when the *hambatsu* intervened in the judicial process to attempt to secure the death sentence for the policeman, Tsuda Sanzō, who had attempted to assassinate Crown Prince Nicholas of Russia. The primary issue in that crisis was the sole right of judges to determine what law should be applied and to apply it without interference from executive officials and without regard to political considerations, however grave. The test was the clearest possible. The oligarchy's intervention was not prompted by the personal whims of executive officials, nor by political convenience, nor even by considerations involving cherished *hambatsu* policies. The stake seemed rather to be the very existence of the nation. When the independence of the judiciary prevailed in spite of the awesome risk of war, it was likely to survive almost any test, and in the limited sense of the integrity of the judge or judges in deciding specific cases, it did so, its slight spirit remaining throughout even the tumultuous 1930's.[2]

As the sorry history of individual rights in prewar Japan demonstrates, although judicial independence is essential to the existence of the rule-of-law, it is not in itself sufficient. The victim of unjust laws, brutal police procedures, or the arbitrary and political decisions of the procurator-general may not be much comforted by the knowledge that when he appeared in the courtroom he was tried and sentenced only according to law and by a judge or judges who were immune to political pressure and scrupulous in their application of the law without regard to extraneous factors. Nonetheless, when these principles of the rule-of-law triumphed in the dramatic confrontation between justice and expediency in the Otsu trial in May 1891, a solid though narrow foundation for the later development of constitutionalism was laid in the indigenous tradition.

The Otsu or Konan affair began with the attempted assassination of Russian Crown Prince Nicholas by a policeman, Tsuda Sanzō, as the prince's entourage prepared to leave Otsu to return to Kyoto after a morning of sightseeing and ceremony in and around that lovely city on the shores of Lake Biwa. The new Matsukata government, indeed the oligarchy as a whole, believed the diplomatic crisis could only be averted by imposition of the death sentence. The pressure exerted by the oligarchs on the judges of both the Otsu court and supreme court was very great indeed. *On* and *giri* were invoked along with *han* loyalties and other personal bonds. Threats were utilized: martial law would be declared or an imperial ordinance promulgated if the judges refused to serve the national interest as defined by the oligarchy. The judges were reminded of the emperor's own deep alarm as he viewed the possible consequences of the attack on Nicholas. Every newspaper reinforced their impression of the intensity of popular indignation against Tsuda, who had sullied the national honor and endangered the nation. When the judges voted six to one, on May 27, 1891, in favor of life imprisonment, it was in the face of the dreadful knowledge that a disastrous war might result.

That the six judges allowed no such considerations to deter them from a just decision was due in large part to the influence of their chief justice, Kojima Iken, whose own record of the Otsu affair reveals the very considerable extent to which he had internalized the alien concept of the rule-of-law and, as a consequence, had arrived at a clear formulation of his role and that of his fellow judges as the independent judiciary established by the Meiji constitution, and indeed considered it essential to constitutional government.[3]

Born in 1837, Kojima did not belong to that later generation of samurai leaders who studied abroad during Japan's enlightenment. One of his younger intimates, Hozumi Nobushige, for example, studied at the Middle Temple in London and qualified as a barrister before going on to study in Berlin.[4] Kojima, born a generation earlier, gave illustrious service to the imperial cause before and during the Ishin wars, and went directly from the battlefield into the new bureaucracy, first serving in the Dajōkan and then in 1871 transferring to the new ministry of justice where he remained until he resigned as chief justice in 1892.

It was in the ministry of justice that Kojima's judicial conscience was formed, tested, and tempered, and his insight into the role of law and the judiciary in constitutional government grew and deepened. In 1875-76, for example, the young Kojima defended the principles of law and justice during the Tsurugaoka incident. On that occasion, the Tokyo government stayed its hand for fear of lighting the fuse which led from Tsurugaoka to Satsuma and Saigō to whom many of the Tsurugaoka warriors were personally devoted as well as ideologically committed, but Kojima argued persuasively that such considerations must not deter the application of justice.[5]

Nine years later, Kojima was president of the Osaka court of appeals when the case of Ōi Kentarō and his colleagues came before that court. The *hambatsu* was determined to secure the death sentence under *ex post facto* law promulgated for that purpose. Kojima's decision was nevertheless based on the law in effect at the time of the Ōi conspiracy.[6] Thus he had early made and sustained a commitment to the supremacy of law in the form of judicial independence.

As Pittau has pointed out, and Kojima Iken long before, the Meiji constitution provided in Article 57: "The Judicature shall be exercised by the Courts of Law according to law, in the name of the Emperor," and in his *Commentaries* on the Meiji constitution, Itō Hirobumi himself articulated the principle of judicial independence:

> In ancient times when politics were in a state of primitive simplicity, in no country was the Government distinguished into the judiciary and the administrative. ... As, however, civilization advanced and social affairs became more and more complex, a distinct line of demarkation was drawn between the judiciary and the administrative. The two departments have each different organizations, and neither of them suffers any encroachment upon its sphere of business by the other. In this way, it has been possible to witness great progress in constitutional government.
>
> ... The functions of the administrative are to carry out laws and to take such measures as may be found expedient for the maintenance of the public peace and order, and for the promotion of the happiness of the people, while the duty of the judiciary is to pronounce judgment upon infringements of rights, according to the provisions of the law. In the judiciary, law is everything, and the question of convenience is left out of consideration. In the administrative, however, measures are taken to meet the ever-changing requirements demanded for the convenience and necessities of society; and law simply shows the limits beyond which they are not permitted to obtrude. Such being the distinction between the nature of the administrative and that of the judiciary, were there only administrative officials and no judicial functionaries, the rights of individuals would be in danger of being made subservient to the ends of social convenience and would ultimately be encroached upon by power.
>
> Therefore trials must be conducted according to law; the law is the sole standard for conducting trials, which must always be conducted in a court of law.
>
> ... Though it is in the power of the Sovereign to appoint judges, and though courts of law have to pronounce judgment in the name of the Sovereign, yet the Sovereign does not take it upon Himself to conduct trials, but causes independent courts to do so, in accordance to law and re-

gardless of the influence of the administrative. Such is what is meant by the independence of the judiciary.[7]

Nonetheless, just two years later Itō participated in the *hambatsu*'s effort to secure Tsuda's execution. One assumes that he justified himself in doing so with the thought that in this case the very physical existence of the nation might be imperiled. Faced with the fearsome possibility of a dreadful war, Itō was willing to consider any means by which Tsuda Sanzō might be "legally" executed, balking only when Mutsu and Gotō proposed that the government hire an assassin to arrange Tsuda's death.[8] Despite his lengthy elucidation of the principle of judicial independence in the *Commentaries,* Itō's role in the Otsu affair suggests that his commitment was to rule-by-law, not the rule-of-law.

The choice as it was presented by the Otsu crisis was between application of the law at the risk of war or sacrifice of the rule-of-law for the sake of the national security. Faced with the dilemma Itō himself had suggested when he wrote the above passage in his *Commentaries,* Kojima applied the principle Itō had articulated and then repudiated.

The chief justice was by no means alone in his defense of the rule-of-law. Initially, the judges of the supreme court all supported his position and although some vacillated later as they were subjected to extreme pressure, in the end Tsuda was sentenced to life imprisonment by a vote of six to one. The functionaries of the ministry of justice fought Minister of Justice Yamada to a standstill in a spirited three-hour oral battle on May 12. Highly respected scholars of jurisprudence such as Hozumi Nobushige gave Kojima their moral and professional support, and many of the small number of practicing lawyers rallied round as the crisis mounted. Indeed, one of the significant aspects of the Otsu affair is the degree to which it both revealed and contributed to the professionalization of the judiciary and the differentiation of both legal and judicial roles.

The judges also received strong political support. Prince Konoe had been much influenced by English constitutional history and theory while studying abroad. Surely the story of Coke's historic confrontation with James I in Whitehall had been part of that political education. By 1891, he was already emerging as a leader of the nonparty anti-*hambatsu* forces in the Diet. He was greatly exercised by the Otsu affair and, after it was over, led a movement in the upper house to censure the government, charging, "This is an invasion of the judicial power by the executive, and is a distortion not to be permitted in constitutional government."[9]

One of the most eloquent statements of the necessity of living by the rule-of-law, even in the extraordinary, dangerous circumstances of May 1891, came from the opposition newspaper *Nihon,* which published on May 17, 1891, an article declaring that if Tsuda were to be judged on the basis of the heinous nature of his act and the outrage felt by patriotic Japanese, no punishment would be too severe: "However, Japan has law, it has courts, it has judges. Criminals, whether their crimes are great or small, grave or trivial, all are judged by the court which has jurisdiction according to the judges. . . . There is no criminal law by which men can be judged except the statutory law. Therefore, no matter how heinous the crime, . . . not even the slightest encroachment by others must be permitted. The statutory law must not be distorted by farfetched interpretations for the sake of other considerations."

On May 17, 1891, the least perceptive reader of *Nihon* would have recognized the reference to the Otsu affair, but the writer proposed to leave nothing to chance. He went on to refer explicitly to the forthcoming trial of Tsuda, saying, "Therefore, we hope our judges will forthrightly defend our statutory law and refrain from taking into account any other circumstances at all."[10] For its audacity in defense of the rule-of-law, *Nihon* paid, first with censorship, then with suspension, all very legally under the rule-by-law.

It was in this atmosphere that the judicial conscience of prewar Japan was formed. In a popular and elite climate of opinion that came close to panic regarding the possibility of war with Russia, seven judges hesitated, several indeed vacillating for sixteen days. Nonetheless, in the end, on May 27, 1891, when the moment came to hand down a decision in the case of Tsuda Sanzō, six out of seven judges voted for life imprisonment. They had indeed vacillated, but in the circumstances it may be understandable that they paused when the price of their integrity might well have been the physical extinction of the nation. The leadership came from Kojima Iken, whose commitment to the rule-of-law began long before the crisis and continued, undiminished, throughout it. Together the six and the one have provided a tradition which legitimizes in post-World War II Japan the otherwise alien concepts of judicial independence and the supremacy of law.

Crown Prince Nicholas began his tour of the East in late 1890, when he left home for Austria and then Greece, where he was joined in his travels by Prince George. Together, the two princes, Russian and Greek, aged twenty-five and twenty-three respectively, journeyed to India, Siam, and China. Finally, on April 27, 1891, the Russian warship on which they traveled anchored in the harbor of Nagasaki. The party planned to spend the month of May in Japan, traveling from Nagasaki and Kagoshima in Kyushu to Aomori in northern Honshu. In Tokyo, the crown prince was to be the honored guest at ceremonies celebrating the completion of Nicolai Cathedral. This appearance and his presence in the Russian Far East when the eastern end of the Trans-Siberian Railroad was commenced constituted the official justification for his journey. No doubt Nicholas' government and parents also regarded the tour as part of the education of the prince who would one day be czar.[11]

The crown prince's grand tour of the East seemed to many Japanese more likely to be a part of a great Russian design for encompassing Eastern Asia. With the beginning of the Trans-Siberian Railroad and the crown prince's visit to Japan, the ancient menace of Russia assumed a form apparent to the man in the street and cabinet member alike. More than one Japanese was sure that all the elaborate sightseeing in fact masked an assessment of Japan's defenses.

The European princes arrived in Kobe harbor on May 9 and went to Kyoto late that afternoon. It was a lovely season in which to visit Japan, and their hosts had spared no effort in arranging for their pleasure. Prince Arisugawa himself superintended arrangements and accompanied them on their travels. The visiting princes spent May 10 sightseeing in Kyoto, seeing many things familiar to most tourists in the famous city as well as treasures reserved for the sight of only the most honored guests.

Early the morning of the eleventh, Nicholas and George left their Kyoto inn, the Tokiwa, in a long and colorful rickshaw procession. The route to Otsu was gaily decorated; the flags of Russia, Greece, and Japan flew everywhere; fireworks brightened the sky. When the princes reached the border of Shiga prefecture, its governor greeted them and joined their party, escorting them to Miidera to enjoy its magnificent view of Lake Biwa.

The last stage of the little journey to Otsu was by boat. On arrival in the lakeshore city, the party went to the prefectural office for the inevitable welcoming ceremonies and luncheon in the meeting hall. About 1:30 that afternoon the procession formed to begin its return to Kyoto.[12]

Tsuda Sanzō was one of the policemen on duty at a street corner where the procession would pass on its return to the old capital city. The thirty-seven-year-old former samurai from Iga had attended the *han* school, and when the *han* were abolished went with his classmates to the Nagoya garrison, first as a common soldier, then as a noncommissioned officer. He fought ably and bravely against the Satsuma rebels and then left the army in 1882. In 1884, Tsuda became a policeman, first in Mie prefecture and finally in Shiga where on May 4, 1891, he was assigned to guard duty in Otsu during the European princes' stay in Kansai.[13]

From his youth Tsuda had harbored a dread and suspicion of Russia. Such incidents as the 1875 exchange in which Russia took Sakhalin and Japan took the Kurile Islands seemed to him to be entirely to Russia's advantage. With the beginning of the Trans-Siberian Railroad and Nicholas' visit to Japan, the menace took shape. Tsuda did not believe for a minute that the Russian crown prince had come to Japan merely to see the dancers of Gion or to be refreshed by Miidera's view of Lake Biwa, and he was appalled at the prospect of the spy's reception at court by the Emperor Meiji. On duty in the precincts of Miidera temple the morning of May 11, Tsuda dwelt on the past and the future, and when two Europeans came to his post and surveyed the district's famous sights as pointed out by their rickshaw bearers, Tsuda thought perhaps the younger one was the Russian prince, setting about the real purpose of his visit. Fortunately for Miidera's two unknown guests, Tsuda let the moment pass, preferring to wait for an occasion when he could be sure of the identity of his victim. Thus there was never any doubt that the Otsu attack was premeditated.[14]

There was never any suggestion that others were implicated in Tsuda's action. The attack was the private deed of a distraught patriot, who was never applauded for his act of sacrifice, as were so many other perpetrators of violence in the name of patriotism in prewar Japan. Rather Tsuda was vilified by his countrymen since, in the national climate of hysterical Russophobia, he appeared to have threatened the very existence of Japan itself.

When the crown prince's rickshaw reached his post along the return route through the Otsu streets, Tsuda saluted, then pursued it, drew his sword, and slashed twice from the right at the prince's head. Nicholas jumped down from his rickshaw to the left, holding his right hand to his wounds, and tried to escape, followed by his assailant. Young Prince George leaped from his rickshaw and ran to Nicholas' aid, beating Tsuda on the back with a bamboo whip. One of the princes' bearers seized Tsuda's legs and pulled him down, another picked up his fallen sword and struck at his back and neck. When Police Chief Kimura hurried back from the head of the procession and ordered him arrested and bound, Tsuda was saved, only to die of pneumonia in a Hokkaido prison less than five months later. The injured prince was given first aid in Otsu; late that afternoon he was returned by train to Kyoto and carried to his rooms at the Tokiwa where Russian doctors, rushed to the scene by special train from Kobe, took over his care.

The officials involved flashed their separate messages to their superiors in Tokyo. Meiji Tennō's court knew the ominous news by 2:30 P.M. Court, government, and public were at once seized by apprehension, even panic, regarding the reaction of mighty Russia. Nishimura Shigeki described the national consternation: "... when the incident became known, the whole country shook with fear. Some said the Crown Prince was dead. Others said his wounds were grave and his life was in doubt. There were all kinds of rumors and the public became more and more agitated."[15] Though it soon became known that Nicholas' wounds were slight, for the next sixteen days the diplomatic aspects of the crisis dominated the thoughts and actions of most of those concerned.

All that was customary, and more, must be done to assure the Russians of Japan's profound regret. That very afternoon the emperor dispatched Prince Kitashirakawa to Kyoto as his personal representative at the bedside of the future czar. In the evening, Home Minister Saigō and Foreign Minister Aoki left for Kyoto accompanied by the army surgeon general. Other delegations, official and unofficial, prepared to carry their apologies and the nation's to the crown prince and his party. Nishimura himself, as president of the peeresses' school, hastened off to Kansai, as did Harai Takuzō representing the Tokyo law academy and Konoe Atsumaro from the upper house of the Diet.[16] The management of Shimbashi Station must have been hard-pressed to meet the requirements of the greatly increased flow of traffic to Kansai, much of it requiring special trains and very special courtesy.

During that first afternoon, an imperial conference met at the palace. Messages went out summoning those who were not in town. Itō and Inoue Kaoru, for example, were vacationing after the extended and elaborate machinations which had accompanied the establishment of the Matsukata cabinet just a few days before. Both genro hurried to Tokyo, Itō arriving at 1:00 A.M. at Shimbashi where he was met by a carriage sent by the palace and carried at once to see the emperor in the imperial bedchamber.

Early the morning of May 12, those members of the cabinet who were still in Tokyo, the genro, court officials, and Chief Justice Kojima, were among those gathered at Shimbashi Station to see the emperor himself off to Kyoto. The atmosphere in the station was sombre, the sky was darkened by a drizzling rain, and members of the assemblage, many of whom thought Japan would be at war when Meiji Tennō returned to his capital, wept as they watched the imperial train pull out of the station.

Now that the customary, almost instinctive, and very necessary courtesies had been set in motion, court and government assessed Japan's position and came to two conclusions as to remedial measures to be undertaken at once. Japan's diplomatic position would be greatly improved if the crown prince were to convalesce at the Tokiwa and to continue his tour, particularly if he were to visit the capital city and be received at the palace by the emperor as originally planned. It was also essential to assuage the anger of Russia and improve Japan's bargaining position by executing Tsuda Sanzō. If these objectives could be accomplished, Russia's retaliation might be less severe.

Early on the twelfth the members of the government and the genro hurried from Shimbashi to the prime minister's official residence to discuss the further steps to be taken. In the hysteria of May 12, 1891, they laid aside the preoccupation with treaty revision and Japan's "image" in the eyes of the treaty powers, which for twenty-three years had prevailed over almost every other consideration. The good opinion of no other foreign power mattered now; only St. Petersburg counted in the deliberations. The constitutional principle of judicial independence so nobly elaborated by Itō in his *Commentaries* was abandoned. Only Mutsu Munemitsu spoke for constitutionalism when he urged the life sentence provided for those who attempted the murder of ordinary persons; and this brief impulse was stilled by Inoue Kaoru's eloquent arguments in favor of the political and expedient execution of Tsuda Sanzō.[17] The participants therefore agreed unanimously that no effort must be spared to secure the death sentence, and the meeting broke up, each member departing to perform his assigned role in Tsuda's execution.

Itō himself rushed off to prepare to leave for Kyoto where he had been instructed to join the emperor by the next train. His primary function in Kansai would be diplomatic contacts with the Russians, first of all in the hope of persuading Nicholas to remain at the Tokiwa until he recovered and then to complete his scheduled tour of Japan. He would also participate there in the numerous conferences designed to further the execution of Tsuda.[18]

When he left Shimbashi that morning after the departure of the emperor's train, the new chief justice of the supreme court, Kojima Iken, also hurried to the prime minister's official residence, accompanied by his successor as president of the Osaka court of appeals, Kitabatake Harafusa. There, after the government's breakfast conference adjourned, Matsukata and Mutsu received the two judges. As Kojima himself recalled the conversation, the constitutional issue at once became explicit. The prime minister explained why the government felt it was essential to execute Tsuda and said that the cabinet, even including the minister of justice, Yamada, had therefore decided on the death sentence in accord with Article 116 of the criminal code which provided for that penalty for anyone who committed violence against the emperor, empress, or crown prince. Mutsu elaborated on the cabinet's position, arguing that since the text of Article 116 referred simply to the "emperor," its provisions did not apply merely to the emperor, empress and crown prince of Japan, but to those of foreign countries as well. Thus this first confrontation revealed that the constitutional aspect of the crisis was going to revolve around the question of who should determine what law should be applied, while a secondary argument would rage over the applicable law.

Kojima dealt forthrightly with both issues, declaring, "Whatever the cabinet has discussed and decided, I [as chief justice of the supreme court] cannot agree to any interpretation contrary to the spirit of the law." The cabinet's interpretation of Article 116 was just that. When the Genrō In had revised the penal code in 1880, the word "Japanese" had been omitted from Article 116 because the word used for emperor was "Tennō" which could only refer to the emperor of Japan. Use of the adjective "Japanese" would therefore have been redundant. "The intent [of the revision]," he pointed out, "was not at all to broaden the scope of application." The prime minister responded that this might be so, but was not legalism irrelevant when the existence of the nation was at stake? "The nation's existence comes before that of the law," he said. "If there is no nation, there will be no law."[19]

Troubled, though not in conscience, Kojima left the prime minister for the ministry of justice where he found Minister of Justice Yamada engaged in legal disputation with the staff and already besieged. The legal question at issue was again the applicability of Article 116. With the greatest earnestness, Yamada urged the government's position. The purpose of the criminal law was primarily to preserve the tranquility and order of the nation. The reason for distinguishing between crimes against ordinary persons and those against the imperial family was not merely to preserve the latter's exalted dignity but also because crimes against them threatened the peace and order of the nation. In this respect there was no difference between acts of violence directed toward the Japanese imperial family and those committed by Japanese subjects against the monarchs of foreign countries or members of their families. Since Article 116 used only the phrase "Tennō oyobi Sankō Kōtaishi," unqualified by the adjective "Japanese," there was no obstacle to the application of Article 116 in the case of the attempted assassination of the Russian crown prince. Officials of the ministry of justice refuted these arguments in the same manner Kojima had employed not long before in conference with Matsukata and Mutsu. When the meeting broke up three hours later, no minds had been changed.[20]

On the next day, May 13, Kojima met with the judges of the supreme court and raised with them the question of the proper interpretation of Article 116. They too were unanimous; the word "Tennō" meant the emperor of Japan, no other. When Kojima so informed the minister of justice that afternoon, the latter responded with the bluff the government was to use repeatedly for the next fourteen days: "If the judges . . . adhere only to the letter of the law and do not change their stubborn view, we will . . . in the end be unable to entrust these grave matters of state to the judges and it will be necessary to handle the matter as an emergency by declaring martial law."[21]

On the same day the Otsu trial court notified the chief justice that it proposed to try Tsuda as though his crime had been against any ordinary person, that is, under Articles 292 and 112 which provided for the death sentence for premeditated murder and reduction of that sentence by one or two degrees when the premeditated murder was attempted but not completed. In reply, Kojima urged that the Otsu court proceed at once to trial. In view of what Yamada had said about martial law, it was clear that the interests of justice would best be served by quick action before the cabinet could intervene further.

Yamada immediately dispatched the procurator-general, Miyoshi Taizō, to Kansai. Although Miyoshi believed that Article 116 was not applicable and privately argued this point with Yamada and other members of the government, he complied with the minister's orders and the ordeal of the Otsu judges began.

In Kansai that day each event heightened the government's alarm. Those who called on the Russian ambassador found his attitude threatening. The security arrangements had been deplorable from the beginning; now he feared for the safety of all his countrymen throughout Japan.[22]

Late in the morning of the thirteenth, the emperor himself called on the crown prince, who was magnanimous, telling Meiji Tennō, as he told all who called on him, that what had occurred in Otsu had not in the least altered his warm feelings for Japan. This made for a pleasant and gracious conversation, no doubt, but his visitors would have been relieved to hear that his warm feelings would cause Nicholas to convalesce at the Tokiwa and then to continue his tour. Instead, not long after the emperor returned to the palace from the Russians' inn, the crown prince sent the dreaded word that his parents had instructed him to remove at once to the Russian warship in Kobe harbor. The Russian ambassador turned the screw once more when he insisted that the emperor accompany the crown prince to Kobe in order to ensure the latter's safety on the journey. Court and government leaders flinched, but the emperor consented and the move was accomplished without incident in the late afternoon of May 13. Such were the consequences of the deed of the policeman who had been appalled at the prospect of the crown prince's ceremonial reception at the court of the emperor in Tokyo!

As alarm mounted in Kansai, the government increased its pressure on the Otsu judges and intensified its diplomatic efforts. The court decided to send Prince Arisugawa to Russia as the head of an official mission carrying Japan's profound apologies to the Russian court, government, and people. Meanwhile, Itō and others redoubled their efforts to persuade the crown prince to complete his scheduled visit to Japan, and particularly to accept the emperor's hospitality in Tokyo.

When an imperial conference convened at the palace in Kyoto on May 15, the participants explored in detail the possibility of an imperial ordinance. Foreign Minister Aoki had prepared a draft which provided *ex post facto* for the death penalty for those who committed acts of violence against foreign chiefs of state or members of their families. That project was dropped for the moment when privy council chief secretary, Itō Miyoji, vigorously opposed it, but there was no lessening of the resolve to see Tsuda dead.[23]

On the following day, May 16, the Russian crown prince informed the emperor by letter that his parents wished him to convalesce in the Russian Far East before attending the ceremonies celebrating the eastern commencement of the Trans-Siberian Railroad. Nicholas would therefore depart from Japan on May 19. The shocked emperor responded that he would personally travel to Kobe on the nineteenth in order to say farewell and he invited the prince to meet him ashore for that occasion. For a brief interval it appeared that the invitation would be accepted, but word soon came that the prince's doctors had vetoed any departure from the ship. Nicholas therefore courteously invited Meiji Tennō to come aboard for luncheon. Nowhere in Japan's history was there any precedent for the emperor to visit the ship of a foreign government, and the occasion hardly seemed propitious for the inauguration of a new practice. It is a measure of the degree of panic within the government that some immediately had visions of the Russian warship steaming out of Kobe harbor, bearing the Meiji Emperor off to St. Petersburg as hostage. Itō pronounced this nonsense. Since Russia was a civilized country, the risks involved in accepting the luncheon invitation were nothing as compared with the consequences which might follow refusal. The emperor therefore accepted the Russian invitation, but many would be anxious until Meiji Tennō was safely back on the Kobe pier on the afternoon of May 19.[24]

When Itō Hirobumi and Inoue Kaoru called on the Russian ambassador that day in Kobe, he said nothing to relieve the growing tension. Itō speculated aloud on the possibility that Tsuda might be sentenced to life imprisonment rather than to death and was at once given to understand that Russia would not regard that outcome as satisfactory.[25]

The same day an imperial ordinance was promulgated providing for prior censorship of all materials regarding foreign affairs. The ordinance served a dual purpose. It made it possible for the government to prevent the publication of articles that might stimulate further incidents or expressions of hostility toward the Russians. Now that the constitutional aspect of the crisis was reaching its climax, and the moment approached when someone must sentence Tsuda, the ordinance also gave the government an invaluable political advantage in the struggle against the judges since it could be used to prevent the publication of materials that would mobilize support on the side of the judiciary.[26]

In these circumstances of panic and pressure, the Otsu trial court on May 18 concluded its preliminary hearing with the finding that Article 116 was the applicable law; this being so, the Tsuda case was not within its jurisdiction. Under the law, the supreme court must now establish a special court to try Tsuda Sanzō, and on the eighteenth the constitutional struggle was transferred from Kansai to the ministry of justice in Tokyo.

Early that morning in Tokyo, Matsukata called Kojima to an emergency conference. Today this in itself strikes a warning note, but in the circumstances of Japan in 1891, very early in its experience with the practice of judicial independence, the chief justice went at once to the prime minister who greeted him with an implied threat. Was the position he understood to be Kojima's in fact the view of the entire court? he asked. The question presaged the *hambatsu*'s tactics in the next few hours and indeed, the next nine days. Kojima immediately replied that he could speak only for himself as the chief justice of the supreme court.

The prime minister at once produced the appeal most likely to secure the compliance of any Japanese. On the morrow the emperor himself would confront the Russians. The government was understandably anxious, considering the unfavorable circumstances in which the meeting would take place. The difficulty of the emperor's position was greatly increased by the probability that the Russians would ask some specific questions regarding Tsuda's future. When the visit of the crown prince had been first discussed by the two governments, the Russian ambassador had suggested that it might be wise to issue an imperial ordinance since the Japanese law contained no explicit provision regarding attacks on the heads of foreign states or members of their families. The foreign minister had replied that there was no need for such action since, if the totally unexpected disaster occurred, it would be dealt with under the law regarding such occurrences affecting the Japanese imperial family. Moreover, after the attempted assassination, Foreign Minister Aoki, acting in accord with the cabinet's decision that Japan must not go back on its word, had told the Russian ambassador that Article 116 would be the law applied, and the home minister had informed the prefectures to the same effect. What then was the emperor to say if he were questioned tomorrow? If the court were unreasonable, there would be no course for the government to take other than the declaration of martial law to be applied retroactively.

These complications caught the chief justice by surprise. Both foreign minister and home minister had acted unconstitutionally, and there was no doubt that in doing so they had created a situation of great potential embarrassment for the emperor and the nation. Still, he reflected in his memoirs, "was not this the responsibility of the members of the cabinet? The responsibility of the judiciary is simply to adhere to the spirit of the law." Nonetheless, Kojima hesitated a while before answering, troubled by the burden that would be his if the emperor were indeed sharply questioned by his hosts.

When he finally replied, he explained that though he was chief justice, he would not be participating in the trial of Tsuda, which would be conducted by a special court in accordance with the provisions of the law. He went on to discuss the legal points at issue. Since he and the prime minister had conferred on May 12, he said, he had explored European and American precedents and had found that while there were some for special treatment involving foreign chiefs of state, there were none where crown princes or other members of ruling families were concerned. In Russia itself there was no death penalty except for injury to the emperor or treason.

To apply 116 to the monarchs of foreign countries and their families would without a doubt be a violation of Japan's sovereignty. It would invite the ridicule and scorn of foreigners familiar with the law and the regret of generations still to be born. [Whatever the feelings aroused by Tsuda's act] we must understand that the law is the spirit of the nation and judges must not act on the basis of their personal feelings. What would happen if they were to do so? They would be in fact untrue to their responsibilities and their disloyalty and infidelity to the nation would have the result of causing the august Emperor to abuse his sacred sovereignty. Therefore, no matter what the danger to the nation, those who are judges can only rely on the exact words of the law and so safeguard its spirit.[27]

After Kojima had also dismissed the possibility of martial law as being both inappropriate and, as *ex post facto* law, unconstitutional, Matsukata turned to a technique described by the chief justice as "when shooting at the enemy, shoot first at the horse." The prime minister said in effect that it was plain that it was the view of the seven judges that would count in the end, not the legalisms of the chief justice who could do little to interfere. Who would the seven be, he asked? Kojima took up a pen and wrote down their names: President Tsutsumi Masami, Haji Tsunesuke, Yasui Shūzō, Inoue Masakazu, Takano Saneson, Kinoshita Tetsusaburō, Naka Sadamasa.[28]

Kojima left the prime minister shortly before noon. While at lunch he learned that at noon Minister of Justice Yamada, Minister of Education Oki, and Minister of Agriculture Mutsu had appeared at the supreme court, calling for Tsutsumi, Naka, Takano, and Kinoshita, who had answered the summons. Each of the emperor's ministers had talked to the judge or judges on whom he could expect to exercise the greatest influence: Mutsu to Tsutsumi, Yamada to Naka, Oki to Takano, Yamada and Judge Kurizuka to Kinoshita. Haji, or so the ministers thought, was theirs since he was a Satsuma man with close links to Saigō.[29] Yasui and Inoue had no friends in the cabinet and were known to be committed to opposing the government.[30] Four votes were needed to execute Tsuda, and therefore three of the four whom the ministers summoned must be persuaded by appeals to reason, self-interest, or loyalty.[31]

At two that afternoon Kojima received a telegram from Procurator-General Miyoshi requesting the appointment of a hearing commissioner to conduct the preliminary examination necessary before trial by the special court. The request was in line with the law, and Kojima accordingly transmitted it to Tsutsumi, who convened his colleagues. Kojima was then requested by them to appoint a commissioner, and he named Doi Yōtarō of the Otsu court.

Doi's report was received by telegram at ten o'clock the night of the eighteenth. To no one's surprise, and certainly not Kojima's, the commissioner found Article 116 to be the applicable law in this case of the premeditated attempted assassination of Crown Prince Nicholas.[32] While Kojima waited alone in his chambers composing the memorandum he proposed to deliver to the prime minister and minister of justice on May 19, the seven judges met and in the early hours of the nineteenth notified Kojima that they would constitute themselves the special court to try Tsuda: Tsutsumi, Naka, Haji, Yasui, Inoue, Takano, and Kinoshita. Of these only Yasui and Inoue could be expected to adhere to the position all seven had agreed to on May 13. The struggle seemed to be all but over, with expediency bound to prevail over the law. Kojima recorded his despair: "When I received this document [notification of the establishment of the special court], I knew for the first time the full extent of what had occurred in those conversations between the ministers and the four judges. Personal feelings had prevailed even over the law which is the life of the nation . . . . The rights and obligations of Japanese citizens and the sacred independence of the judicial power would in the future be destroyed thanks to the judges' weakness of will and purpose."[33]

Kojima could have taken only small comfort from the news that the emperor's visit to the Russian warship had concluded without incident. The conversation between the emperor and crown prince had been pleasant. The embarrassing questions had not been asked; indeed, the Russians had assured Meiji Tennō that there was no need to dispatch the Arisugawa mission to St. Petersburg. The emperor had safely returned to his palace in Kyoto. One wonders if the Russians were unaware of the state of the Japanese nerves, or if kindness prevented them from finding it necessary to shift the position of their ship ever so slightly sometime during the luncheon party.

While government and court officials in Kansai and Tokyo

had waited anxiously for news of the emperor's visit with the
Russians, Kojima spent much of the day in completion of the
memorandum which he hoped would cause the cabinet to recon-
sider. During the day his old friend and junior clansman from
Uwajima, the distinguished jurist Hozumi Nobushige, came to
call. He gave his stout support to the draft in preparation,
greatly heartening the chief justice. Later, Soyeda Juichi, private secretary to Matsukata, asked for an interview and was most
encouraging. Late in the afternoon, the chief justice delivered
his memorandum to Matsukata and Yamada, and at 9:50 the
evening of the nineteenth he left Shimbashi Station for Kansai,
accompanied by the seven judges who would try the case of
Tsuda.

The judges of the nation's highest court stopped in Kyoto
on the way to Otsu, summoned there to an audience with the
emperor. The imperial edict was an admonition to proceed at
once and "with care" to settle the crisis which threatened the
nation. The phrase "with care" was ambiguous: it could have
been a warning not to tamper with the new constitution; it
could as well have been a reminder of the awful risk of war.
Kojima went directly to Imperial Household Minister Hijikata
in the hope of enlightenment, but he was told only that the
imperial message had been worded correctly. He and everyone
else remained free to interpret the emperor's will as suited his
purpose.[34]

With Tsuda's trial by a special court scheduled for May 25,
the chief justice found himself handicapped by the very law he
had sworn to defend. Since he was not himself a member of the
special court there was little he could properly do to intervene.
Fully conscious of the limits of judicial propriety, he may well
have gone beyond them in the end.[35] He met with Tsutsumi on
the twenty-first for a private and forthright conversation in their
Otsu inn. The chief justice told the junior judge quite frankly
how he saw the stakes in the crisis: the issue was a matter not
only of his and Tsutsumi's honor and that of the judiciary col-
lectively, but also the honor of the emperor and the nation. In
his argument, he used the ambiguous words of the imperial rescript to advantage: "The words *'chūi shite'* [with care] were
the main point and spirit of the rescript and we must not over-
look them!" Kojima himself interpreted the emperor's command
as requiring him to oppose the cabinet with every means possible,
"for the sake of the honor of the nation and the authority of the

constitution." Tsutsumi now must choose between the personal considerations invoked by the ministers on the eighteenth and the requirements of justice and constitutionalism. "Indeed," Kojima admonished him, "the outcome of the nation's crisis depends upon what you and your colleagues do."[36]

Kojima handed Tsutsumi a copy of the memorandum he had delivered on the nineteenth to Matsukata and Yamada and begged him to read it carefully. He himself was going to Osaka on business. He could be reached there and would return at once if Tsutsumi wished. Kojima regarded this interview as his final effort.

The chief justice went to each of the judges to say goodbye and left for Osaka by train at four that afternoon, seen off at the station by Tsutsumi. It was an emotional parting in view of both men's knowledge of the gravity of the issue which would be decided before they met again. For his part, Kojima appreciated Tsutsumi's dilemma and sympathized.[37] All now depended on Tsutsumi's resolution of his own conflict. While the chief justice's appeal had been a moving one, Tsutsumi must have considered the wrath of the *hambatsu* should he give way, and far more serious, he must have contemplated what it would be like to be known by himself and all others as the man who had insisted on judicial independence and thus brought on his country a terrible war and perhaps extinction of the nation.

The document Kojima left with Tsutsumi had been written in the hope of influencing the *hambatsu*. It had more effect in shaping the decision of Tsutsumi; its largely legal and constitutional argument served to recall Tsutsumi to his role as a member of the judiciary under the Meiji constitution. In his memorandum, the chief justice discussed once more the inapplicability of Article 116 to the rulers of foreign states and members of their families. He reviewed the laws of foreign countries and found that even if the ordinary law were applied to Tsuda, his punishment, a life sentence, would be more severe than that provided in Western penal codes for such offenses. If Articles 23 and 57 of the Meiji constitution were violated in Tsuda's case, how could confidence in the law and the integrity of the judicial power be maintained?[38]

Moreover, Kojima appealed to one of the deepest concerns of his countrymen during the Meiji era, the ardent wish for equal status for Japan in the ranks of the great powers, when he argued that if Article 116 were wrongly interpreted to include foreign chiefs of state and members of their families, then the distinction between Japan and other countries would be lost. "Ah," he wrote, "if the nation is not sovereign, how can it be said to be an independent country?" Since "Russia is not at all a barbarian country," there was in fact no reason to suppose it would take advantage of the situation to make unjust and harsh demands on Japan. This being so, would it not be a pity to give the treaty powers an excuse for postponing still further the long-delayed revision of the unequal treaties or even for making new demands? Thus Kojima argued that even from the political point of view, what the government was seeking was unnecessary and would be unwise.[39]

At two o'clock the afternoon of May 23, just two days before Tsuda's trial was to begin, the chief justice, marking time with routine chores in the familiar environment of Osaka, received a telegram from Tsutsumi calling him back to Otsu. The summons was the signal of the beginning of the awakening of the collective judicial conscience and Kojima obeyed at once. The two men conferred late that afternoon in their Otsu inn. Yasui, Inoue, and now Tsutsumi, would do what was right; one more vote was necessary if the rule-of-law were to prevail. By midnight, Kojima, assisted by Yasui, had assured at least two more votes, Kinoshita's and, surprisingly, Haji's, making a certain total of five.[40]

The morning of May 24, Kojima notified Minister of Justice Yamada by telegram that Article 116 would not be applied in Tsuda's case. The cabinet, caught by surprise and confronted with the beginning of the trial the next day, requested a postponement, which was granted by the court. Minister of Justice Yamada and Home Minister Saigō departed for Kansai that afternoon, and their final confrontation with the chief justice began the morning of May 25. Miyoshi, the procurator-general, was also present.

When the legal arguments, by now familiar to all concerned, had been once more exhausted, Yamada asked for the names of the defecting judges; Kojima refused to tell him in order to protect not only the individual judges but also the principle of the confidential nature of the court's proceedings.

Saigō's approach was highly emotional. "I don't know anything about the law," he declared, but if the judges were to proceed as they intended, "not only will the Emperor's will be disobeyed but the Russian fleet will enter Shinagawa harbor and our country will be overthrown. If this happens, we cannot say that the law has protected the nation but rather that it has destroyed the country." Kojima responded indignantly; how could anyone say that the law would destroy the nation when the law was itself "one of the main arteries supporting the life of the nation .... In the eyes of the judiciary, there is only the law."[41]

The emperor was distressed, Saigō reminded the chief justice. Could the judges ignore his wishes? Kojima's conscience was quite clear on this point. The emperor had only instructed the judges "to take care," which was indeed what they were doing; Meiji Tennō's rescript had made no reference to Article 116.

Yamada brought the meeting to an end with a request that he and Saigō be allowed to meet separately with each of the judges. Kojima naturally enough feared a repetition of what had occurred at the ministry of justice on May 18. While he would discuss the justice minister's request with the judges, he made it clear that he would use his influence to persuade them to refuse to meet with Yamada and Saigō. Supported by Yasui and Tsutsumi, Kojima secured the judges' agreement that it would be quite improper to permit those who were bringing charges to meet privately with those who would judge the case. Yamada took the news of their final defeat philosophically, confiding to Kojima that the government's purpose now was not so much to alter the court's decision as to impress the Russians with its sincerity in wishing to make amends for the injury to Nicholas. The distraught Saigō, already drinking heavily, responded with an anger undiminished when Kojima told him that the relationship between the minister of justice and judges was not like that which prevailed between the home minister and prefectural officials: "[Judges] submit only to the law. They have no obligation to submit to the orders of any man."[42]

Tsuda Sanzō's trial began shortly after noon, May 27, in the crowded Otsu courtroom. The now-worn facts and arguments were presented by the procurators and the attorneys representing Sanzō. At three the judges began their deliberations and at six o'clock that evening the sentence of life imprisonment was handed down. Six out of the seven judges had in the end decided that the applicable laws were Articles 292 and 112 of the criminal code, not Article 116. Since Kojima in his scrupulous way did not record it, we do not know who the sixth judge was, Takano Saneson or Naka Sadamasa.[43] Jubilant with what the six had done, the chief justice at once telegraphed the grand news to Hozumi Nobushige who shared it, rejoicing, with his colleagues in Tokyo. The telegram from Otsu was long cherished in Hozumi's home.[44]

At midnight on the twenty-seventh, the chief justice went to the Otsu station to see the ministers off for Tokyo. The leave-taking of the minister of justice and the chief justice was civil, each having done what his role required him to do, but a final embarrassing scene occurred when Kojima parted from the home minister who returned to Tokyo expecting the imminent calamity of war.[45] He was wrong by thirteen years; when war came, it had nothing to do with the attempted assassination of Nicholas; it ended in the victory no one would have hoped for in the spring of 1891. The apprehensions of the Japanese government and public notwithstanding, the Otsu affair was from first to last primarily a constitutional crisis, producing no significant diplomatic consequences. Preoccupied by the prospect of bad harvests and famine at home, and ever-conscious of the logistics problem that would not be finally solved until completion of the Trans-Siberian Railway in 1905, the Russians accepted with an unexpected grace the news that Tsuda's life would be spared. Indeed, the Russian ambassador, whose mischief had added greatly to the crisis atmosphere in Kansai, informed the foreign office that if the sentence had been death, the czar would have requested the emperor to exercise mercy.[46]

Politically, the Otsu affair was no more than another of a long series of incidents used by anti-*hambatsu* forces to harass the government, some like Konoe denouncing its intervention in the judicial process, others like Tani Kanjō attacking it for failure to execute Tsuda.[47] Those ministers most closely identified with the crisis left office; the Matsukata government remained in power until August 1892. When it fell, it fell because the oligarchy found it useful to transfer responsibility to Itō and Chōshū, not because the Matsukata cabinet had mismanaged the security arrangements for the crown prince's visit, had attempted to execute Tsuda, or had failed to do so.

Insignificant in Japan's diplomatic and political history, the Otsu affair was an important episode in Japan's constitutional life. The judicial crisis did a great deal to bring into being a judiciary with high standards of professional conduct and a keen sense of identity and solidarity, and the subsequent role formulation of Japan's judges was to a large extent determined by what happened at Otsu in May 1891. In these ways, the events of the sixteen days of crisis contributed greatly to Japan's legal modernization, since the existence of the modern state would be precarious at best without a professional judiciary.

Constitutionalism or limited government, with its focus on the individual and his rights, would be out of the question if there were no independent judges guarding the constitution and the supremacy of law. True, as much depends on the content of the law and constitution as on the integrity of the judges who apply them. Nonetheless, the post-World War II emphasis on the rights of the individual would be meaningless unless there existed the means to defend them, and the establishment of the tradition of the independent judge was the most lasting and most significant of the consequences of the Otsu Affair.

Although Kojima's record of the contest of wills and conscience through which he had passed in May 1891 gives us no reason to suppose that his dedication to the supremacy of law arose out of consciousness of individual rights as the end and purpose of constitutionalism, his devotion to the law and his definition of his own role as a judge in defense of the supremacy of law were sufficient to assure him a proud place in the history of Japanese constitutionalism. Over and over again during the sixteen days of the Otsu affair, Kojima said to the emperor's ministers in effect what Coke had said to James I in Whitehall in 1608, quoting Henry de Bracton, "The King should be under no man, but under God and the law." In the context of Japan in the spring of 1891, just two years after promulgation of the Meiji constitution and in a climate of Russophobia, Kojima's performance was no minor act of courage, and its consequences reach into the lives of individuals in post-World War II Japan.

NOTES

1. Dan Fenno Henderson, "Law and Political Modernization in Japan," Robert E. Ward, ed., *Political Development in Modern Japan* (Princeton, 1968), pp. 387–456.

2. *Ibid.*, pp. 425–26.

3. Harai Takuzō, ed., *Otsu jiken temmatsuroku* (A detailed record of the Otsu affair; Tokyo, 1931).

4. *Shinsen daijimmei jiten* (Newly selected biographical dictionary; Tokyo, 1938), V, 485.

5. Harada Mitsusaburō, *Kojima Iken den* (The life of Kojima Iken; Matsuyama, 1961), pp. 11–26.
6. *Ibid.*, pp. 43–46; Mori Senzō, ed., *Meiji jimbutsu itsuwa jiten* (An anecdotal dictionary of Meiji personalities; Tokyo, 1965), I, 362, citing Ozawa Shōjirō, *Meiji shinshi tan* (Stories of Meiji gentlemen).
7. Itō Hirobumi, *Commentaries on the Constitution of the Empire of Japan* (Tokyo, 1889), pp. 100–01; Joseph Pittau, *Political Thought in Early Meiji Japan, 1868–1889* (Cambridge, 1967), pp. 192–93.
8. Shunbō Kō Tsuishōkai, *Itō Hirobumi den* (The life of Itō Hirobumi; Tokyo, 1940), II, 758.
9. Konoe Kazan Kai, *Konoe Kazan kō* (Prince Kanoe Kazan; Tokyo, 1924), p. 39, pp. 49–51.
10. *Nihon*, May 17, 1891, "Kyōjin to Keihō" (The assassin and the penal code).
11. Harada, pp. 47–55.
12. *Ibid.*, pp. 55–58.
13. *Otsu jiken temmatsuroku*, pp. 52–53.
14. The text of the report of the judge who conducted the supreme court's preliminary examination is found in *Otsu jiken temmatsuroku*, pp. 51–59. See also Osatake Takeshi, *Konan jiken* (The Konan affair; Tokyo, 1951), p. 112, p. 120.
15. Matsudaira Naosuke, *Hakuō Nishimura Shigeki den* (The life of "Hakuō": Nishimura Shigeki; Tokyo, 1932), II, 50.
16. *Otsu jiken temmatsuroku*, short introduction, p. 9; *Konoe Kazan kō*, p. 49.
17. Harada, pp. 79–80.
18. *Itō Hirobumi den*, II, 747–72.
19. *Otsu jiken temmatsuroku*, pp. 18–24.
20. *Ibid.*, pp. 24–29.
21. *Ibid.*, pp. 27–29.
22. *Itō Hirobumi den*, II, 759.
23. Harada, pp. 85–86.
24. *Itō Hirobumi den*, II, 767–68.
25. *Ibid.*, 764.
26. *Otsu jiken temmatsuroku*, pp. 14–16.
27. *Ibid.*, pp. 41–42.
28. *Ibid.*, pp. 35–44.
29. Harada, p. 93.
30. Unfortunately, a remark concerning Yasui and Inoue was omitted when Kojima's memoirs were edited for publication. *Otsu jiken temmatsuroku*, p. 64.
31. *Ibid.*, pp. 48–51.
32. *Ibid.*, pp. 51–59.
33. *Ibid.*, pp. 62–63.
34. *Ibid.*, pp. 76–78.
35. *Ibid.*, pp. 79–80; Pittau, p. 193, citing Ishii Ryōsuke, *Japanese Legislation in the Meiji Era*, pp. 488–89.
36. *Otsu jiken temmatsuroku*, pp. 80–83.
37. *Ibid.*, p. 85.
38. Article 23 of the Meiji constitution provided, "No Japanese subject shall be arrested, detained, tried or punished, unless according to law." Itō,

Commentaries, p. 46. Article 57 read, "The Judicature shall be exercised by the Courts of Law according to law, in the name of the Emperor." *Ibid.,* p. 100.
39. *Otsu jiken temmatsuroku,* pp. 68-74.
40. Harada, p. 107.
41. *Otsu jiken temmatsuroku,* pp. 97-98.
42. *Ibid.,* p. 106.
43. *Ibid.,* p. 136.
44. *Ibid.,* p. 141.
45. *Ibid.,* pp. 144-47.
46. *Ibid.,* p. 149.
47. Hirao Michio, *Shishaku Tani Kanjō den* (The life of Viscount Tani Kanjō; Tokyo, 1935), pp. 645-46.

The Meiji Model and Chinese Constitutional Reformers

Frank F. Wong
Antioch College

By the end of the nineteenth century, China and Japan had reversed roles in their traditional relationship. The Middle Kingdom, for long the radiating center of cultural diffusion in East Asia, was now on the periphery of modern development. Japan, which had civilized itself by absorbing much of Chinese culture, was the center of a new Asia, revived through the fresh infusion of Western influence. Whereas China had once been the exemplary model for other Asian countries, now Japan showed the way to modernization and equality with the West. It could not have been easy for Chinese leaders to accept this reversal of roles. But Japan's startling successes in the Sino-Japanese War of 1894-95 and the Russo-Japanese War of 1904-05, and China's continuing humiliations before and after the Boxer Uprising in 1899, all helped to undercut the complacent superiority complex of the traditional Chinese.

Chinese observers, searching for the key to the sudden success of Meiji Japan, were most impressed by the political reforms of the Meiji regime. For Confucian-bred Chinese leaders, accustomed to believing that political leadership was the key to the strength and power of a nation, the establishment of a constitutional monarchy was the most persuasive component of the Meiji program. The Meiji constitutional program appealed especially to two groups of reformers that appeared on the Chinese scene in the last decade and a half of the Ch'ing dynasty. Both groups believed constitutional monarchy was the key to Chinese modernization. The first group of radical reformers, emerging from the shock of the Sino-Japanese War, made an abortive effort to achieve their goals under the sponsorship of the Emperor Kuang Hsü in 1898. After the return to power of the empress dowager, these radical reformers were essentially political outsiders, operating clandestinely in China or as exiles in Japan. The second group of conservative reformers, loyal to the empress dowager, somewhat belatedly advocated constitutional reform after the Russo-Japanese War.[1] They were essentially insiders in relation to the imperial throne, and, although they were not all Manchus, they shared a common stake in preserving the shaky authority of the regime. We can obtain some insight into the impact of the Meiji model on these two groups by examining the constitutional thought of Liang Ch'i-ch'ao, a leading spokesman for the outsiders, and of several reformers within the Manchu regime.

Neither Liang nor the Ch'ing reformers advocated uncritical imitation of the Meiji constitution. Yet both, in another sense, advocated imitation of the method by which constitutional reform was introduced to Meiji Japan. In 1900 Liang outlined a program for constitutional development that included sending representatives abroad to study the constitutions of Europe, England, the United States, and Japan.[2] On the basis of such a study, a constitution appropriate for China would be devised. This recommendation followed the precedent of the Itō mission of 1882 in the preparation of the Meiji constitution. Five years later, when the Ch'ing regime decided to implement a program of constitutional reform, they sent two missions to Japan, the United States, England, and Europe for the express purpose of studying the constitutions of these nations.[3] In doing so, they were following not only the procedure recommended by Liang Ch'i-ch'ao (though they would hardly admit to it) but the example of the Meiji experience, with one important difference—they now had the Japanese model to consider in addition to the Western models.

While both Liang and the Ch'ing reformers advocated an eclectic approach to devising a constitution for China, by examining the constitutions of several foreign nations, it is clear that the Meiji example played a large if not dominating role in their constitutional thought. In the 1890's, Liang had learned about the Meiji reforms through Huang Tsun-hsien's History of Japan (Jih-pen kuo-chih) and had come to share Kang Yu-wei's view that China could more quickly and efficiently reform by utilizing the experience of Japan rather than borrowing directly from the West.[4] Later both K'ang and Liang, with the assistance of Japanese legation officials, fled to Japan to escape the empress dowager's coup. While in Japan, Liang enjoyed one of his most productive periods and rapidly became the leading voice for constitutional reform outside the Peking government. In 1906 Liang wrote a series of articles describing the manner in which the Meiji regime had introduced constitutional government in Japan. He applied the lessons of that experience to the Chinese situation. The conservative reformers inside the Ch'ing government were equally impressed and influenced by the Meiji constitutional model. When the constitutional study missions were sent abroad, both groups spent a lengthy period in Japan where they listened to explanations of the Meiji constitution by Prince Itō, the principal architect of the constitution, and by Hozumi Yatsuka,[5] a Tokyo University law professor who advocated absolute loyalty to the emperor. When the commissioners submitted the findings of their study to an imperial commission, they reported that they were impressed by the constitutions of England, Germany, and Japan, but they recommended that the Meiji constitution be used as a model for Chinese constitutional reform.[6]

Although Liang and the conservative Ch'ing reformers were bitter political rivals after 1898, there were a number of reasons why they both shared a common respect for the Meiji constitutional model. Both had come to believe that constitutional government was an essential factor in developing the strength and power of China. The Ch'ing reformers, of course, wished to avoid revolution in order to save their own skins, while Liang feared revolution because he felt it would lead to chaos, weakness, and invasion by the Western powers. Both Liang and the Ch'ing reformers, for different reasons, wished to have political reform within the existing monarchical system and to avoid a republic instituted by revolutionary means. The Meiji experience seemed to suggest that in an Asian nation a constitution within a monarchy was more effective than a constitution within a republic. In brief, both Liang and the Ch'ing reformers saw the Meiji constitutional experience as evidence of the need and proof of the possibility that constitutional monarchy could provide a means of building a more powerful China.

Despite their common esteem for the Meiji constitutional monarchy, however, Liang and the Ch'ing reformers had very different interpretations of the Meiji experience and its application to the Chinese situation. This was especially evident on the issue of imperial authority. The Ch'ing reformers viewed the Meiji constitution as evidence that it was possible to preserve imperial absolutism in the form of constitutional government. In the view of the Ch'ing reformers, the power of the emperor was uncompromised by a constitution. This was a view that was directly transmitted to them by their Japanese consultants, Itō and Hozumi, both of whom held conservative interpretations on the question of imperial authority. Hozumi had advised the Chinese commissioners that the Meiji constitution was based on the total sovereignty of the emperor. Although the constitution slightly altered the means by which the emperor implemented his powers, his sovereignty remained undiminished by the adoption of the Meiji constitution, according to Hozumi. He further explained that the emperor retained the ruling *power* while the parliament, the ministers, and the judiciary represented the ruling *organs,* whose functions were to implement the legislative, executive, and judicial powers that resided in the imperial throne.[7] Itō reiterated this interpretation by denying that the Meiji constitution placed any obstacles in the way of the emperor's powers.[8]

When the members of the constitutional missions made their recommendation to the throne favoring a Meiji-style constitution, they argued that it was desirable because, unlike some constitutions that were forced upon the monarchy by popular demand, the Meiji constitution had been freely implemented by imperial decree.[9] This recommendation seemed to reflect directly the discussion which the commissioners had with Prince Itō. After they had queried Itō on what constitutional model would be most desirable for strengthening China, the Japanese statesman explained that among constitutions there are two basic kinds: those established by the ruler and those established by the people. He advised that since China, like Japan, had long been an imperial nation, it would be best to emulate the Meiji constitution, which had been established by the emperor.[10]

According to Tai Hung-tz'u and Tuan-fang, two other members of the constitutional missions, such imperial constitutions served principally to define the responsibilities of government bodies other than the imperial throne. The absolute authority of the monarch was unchanged by the constitution because his authority transcended the provisions of the constitution.[11] This interpretation of constitutional monarchy was no doubt comforting to the Manchu rulers of China. They had ruled for more than three centuries by Confucian axioms which assumed that the imperial throne was the source of all legitimate authority in the government. Now they were assured that constitutionalism, the key to modern political power, did not threaten their traditional authority.

Other aspects of constitutional government, such as a responsible cabinet and representative assemblies, were also understood by the Ch'ing reformers in terms of their basic assumption that imperial absolutism was preserved in a constitutional monarchy. Tsai-tse noted that Prince Itō had emphasized that supreme power in the government must be retained by the emperor and must not be allowed to fall into the hands of the people.[12] Throughout Itō's discussion with the commissioners, he emphasized the unrestricted powers of the emperor. In response to Tsai-tse's concern about the possible challenge posed by new branches of government created by constitutionalism, Itō assured his Chinese visitor that the powers of the imperial throne remained unimpaired. Parliament could not convene nor dissolve itself without imperial approval, according to Itō. Furthermore, the emperor retained full powers of appointment over all officials responsible for implementing the decisions of the imperial throne. This included ultimate control of the military, said Itō, or else the system would be no different from a republic.[13]

Viewed in this light, a cabinet was interpreted to be a means of facilitating the supreme power of the imperial throne rather than an instrument responsive to elected representatives of the people. According to Tai Hung-tz'u and Tuan-fang, "The function of high government officials is to assist the ruler in the exercise of his governing powers."[14] Insofar as a cabinet was responsible, it was responsible to the imperial throne. The emperor selected the prime minister and the latter organized the cabinet. This cabinet served primarily as a buffer between the ruler and the people, a means of rendering the imperial throne immune from criticism. The main responsibilities of the cabinet ministers were to assume the blame for acts by the imperial throne which might be regarded as unconstitutional by the people and to assume the blame for failures in imperial policy that might encourage discontent among the people. On the other hand, if imperial policy was successful, then the affections of the people, in a constitutional monarchy, would be directed to the imperial throne rather than to cabinet ministers.[15]

In the view of the Ch'ing reformers, representative bodies, like the parliament, were regarded as a useful appendage to the authority of the imperial throne. They might facilitate administrative efficiency but would constitute no threat to the absolute powers of the emperor. Tsai-tse, after his visit to Japan, concluded that "the method of the Japanese government is to let the people share public discussions and the ruler hold political power."[16] This observation seemed to be based on remarks which Hozumi had made to the Chinese commissioners. In discussing the role of parliament, Hozumi had made a distinction between participating in lawmaking and establishing the law. Parliament, he suggested, has the right to discuss and recommend, but the emperor alone has the power to decide and establish law.[17]

Although a parliament might provide a useful expression of trends in public opinion, it should have no legislative power of its own. In the words of another Ch'ing official, a parliament could not contravene the decisions of the imperial throne because the rights of the people "have to do with words only, not with deeds."[18] Curiously, the Ch'ing reformers believed that a parliament could serve to check the powers of the cabinet but not of the emperor. If it pursued the "peoples' interest" at the expense of public administration, however, the emperor should immediately suspend or adjourn the assembly. The primary purpose of involving the people in public affairs was to strengthen the imperial government, not to curtail the powers of the sovereign. The Ch'ing reformers believed that the people would be more dedicated to developing national resources if they participated in government. This would increase the government's tax revenues and also strengthen the government in its dealings with foreign nations.[19]

What the Ch'ing reformers understood to be "constitutional monarchy" was in reality "imperial constitutionalism." Constitutional reforms were to be introduced not to prevent the exercise of arbitrary authority by the imperial throne but to facilitate the strengthening of the nation through the strengthening of the monarchical system. This imperial constitutionalism was summed up in the constitutional regulations issued by the Ch'ing regime in 1910: "It is reverently noted that in the form of constitutional government established by the sovereign, all powers belong to the sovereign making the laws; the executive functions of government and the administration of the laws are all his general prerogatives. In the making of laws, parliament will advise. In the execution of government, the officials will assist. The judges will administer the laws in accordance with statutes."[20] Having understood constitutionalism as a means of strengthening the nation, the Ch'ing reformers, identifying the power of the throne with the power of the nation, assumed it would strengthen the throne as well. The Meiji model was clearly a dominating influence in this interpretation.

The influence of the Meiji model on the constitutional thought of Liang Ch'i-ch'ao was less direct and more complicated. As we indicated earlier, Liang feared revolution and favored reform within the existing system of government in China. Ideally, he would have preferred that a constitutional monarchy be established under the auspices of a sympathetic ruler like the Emperor Kuang Hsü who would listen to the counsel of wise men like himself. Perhaps this hope was inspired by the example of the Meiji emperor. In 1900 Liang called for the voluntary initiation of a constitutional reform program by the emperor. Only in this manner, he wrote, could revolution and chaos be averted.[21] But by this time, the Emperor Kuang Hsü was powerless and Liang was in exile with a price on his head. It was extremely awkward for him to advocate a program of change within the system when he was considered a fugitive by those who dominated the system.

Liang's constitutional views thus came to be colored by the fact that he was an outsider. It was as an outsider that he wrote the three articles on the preparation of the Meiji constitution.[22] This was shortly after the Ch'ing government had announced its intentions to inaugurate a program of constitutional reform. Liang, however, did not use this occasion to praise the Ch'ing rulers for emulating the Meiji emperor. For him, the significance of the Meiji experience was the great influence which "public opinion" exerted upon the framing and adoption of the Meiji constitution. "Public opinion," he noted, did not mean the opinions of the people in general, but those of leading political figures.[23] In his view, such organizations as public societies, political parties, and a free press were the key to constitutional development in Japan. These organizations, by stimulating public discussion of constitutional issues, served as the voice of the people and helped to bring about constitutional reform.

Liang gave special attention to the rise of political parties in Meiji Japan. He made the striking observation that the political parties of Japan had their primary value in the period before the constitution was established rather than afterward.[24] He believed that opposition political leaders were essential to both the establishment of popular rights and the development of political parties. Without opposition leaders like Itagaki, he implied, there might not have been a Meiji constitution. The lesson of the Meiji experience for China was clear. First, the Chinese leaders must develop public opinion as a political force if there is to be genuine constitutional development. Second, Chinese political leaders must emulate Japanese politicians who were willing to resign from office and rally public opinion as opposition leaders.[25] It was not unusual for Liang to draw such conclusions from his study of the Meiji constitutional experience. At the time, he was a prominent opposition leader and an outstanding publicist concerned with shaping public opinion.

The Ch'ing regime had announced its intention to implement voluntarily a constitutional monarchy, much as Liang had originally hoped. But as a distrustful outsider, he was concerned that the Ch'ing program might not embody legitimate constitutional reform. Before, as an insider with access to a sympathetic emperor, he might have placed less emphasis on public opinion. Now, as an outsider, he believed that public pressure was necessary to bring about effective constitutional government. Liang's concerns were well placed. As we have seen, the Ch'ing reformers had a very narrow understanding of constitutionalism based on conservative views of the Meiji constitution. Liang's constitutional thought was more informed and based on a broader understanding of government by law and separation of powers.

In his articles on the making of the Meiji constitution, Liang showed none of the misconceptions about imperial authority that were widely shared among the Ch'ing reformers. He made a clear distinction between imperial absolutism and the limited power of a monarch in a constitutional system. "If you change from authoritarianism to constitutionalism," he wrote, "the influence of those who have held power is restricted, while new power-holders take control."[26] This critical distinction became a favorite theme in Liang's writings as he observed the Ch'ing reformers simulating the appearance of constitutional reform without altering the authority of the imperial throne.

When the Ch'ing Regent Tsai-feng announced the formation of a cabinet in 1911 and then appointed only loyal followers of the imperial throne, Liang was quick to recognize the hollow nature of this reform. The requirement that imperial edicts be countersigned by appropriate cabinet ministers did not provide an effective check upon the authority of the imperial throne in this situation, he noted. This particular Ch'ing reform, in Liang's view, was merely a reversion to the traditional practice of imperial China when members of the Grand Council had signed imperial edicts to authenticate the fact that they came from the emperor and were not forgeries. According to Liang, the critical difference between the so-called cabinet reform of the Ch'ing regime and real constitutional government was that, in the latter, "the minister is responsible to the people and if he believes the edict goes against the will of the people, then he can refuse to sign it." Despite the Ch'ing announcement, Liang noted, China did not yet have a responsible cabinet system.[27]

Liang was also skeptical about the manner in which Ch'ing reformers understood the relationship between parliamentary bodies and imperial authority. In an essay warning people about mistaken views of constitutionalism, he emphasized the difference between the role of the monarch in an autocratic system and his role in a constitutional system: "In autocracy, the power of the monarch is unlimited and he controls the executive, legislative, and judicial functions of government. In a constitutional monarchy, the power of the monarch is limited and the legislative power is exercised by a parliament."[28] Unlike the Ch'ing reformers, he understood the principle of separation of powers and recognized that in an authentic constitutional monarchy, the powers of the sovereign are restricted.

In the context of our present study, we must ask why was there such a discrepancy between the constitutional views of the Ch'ing reformers and Liang Ch'i-chao if they were both inspired by the same Meiji model of constitutional monarchy? We have already noted that Liang and the Ch'ing reformers were attracted to the Meiji model for many of the same reasons. They both thought that constitutional monarchy, Meiji style, would increase the power of China and achieve greater equality with the West. They also believed that it was a means of averting revolution in China and bringing about gradual modernization. But they had very different interpretations of the meaning of the Meiji model for China. The Ch'ing reformers believed that it demonstrated the possibility of retaining imperial absolutism within a constitutional form of government. Liang believed that it demonstrated the possibility of restricting the powers of the imperial throne through rule of law, public opinion, political parties, and the exercise of legislative power by elected representatives of the people.

In part, their differences can be attributed to their respective political positions. The Ch'ing reformers were insiders struggling to preserve the prerogatives which they had long enjoyed and the system which supported those prerogatives. Liang, on the other hand, was an outsider who, despite his instincts for inside political reform, was compelled by circumstances to depend on nontraditional political methods to advance his goals. But this is only part of the story.

Both Liang and the Ch'ing reformers found significance in the Meiji constitutional experience for China's own struggle to adapt itself to modern political institutions. But they brought to their understanding of the Meiji model vastly different backgrounds. Liang had begun his study of Western parliamentary and constitutional government a decade before he wrote his series of articles on the making of the Meiji constitution. Over these years he had become acquainted with Western political theory and had indicated a special interest in British philosophers like Jeremy Bentham and John Stuart Mill. He knew and understood the basic principles of nineteenth-century liberalism and the way in which they were embodied in the British system of constitutional monarchy. As early as 1897 he had written an essay which drew a clear distinction between the unlimited authority of the ruler in a despotism and the limited authority of a monarch in a constitutional system.[29] Thus, when he described Meiji constitutionalism, he read into it his own sympathies for Western liberal constitutionalism.

There is little evidence that the Ch'ing reformers brought any similar intellectual background to their understanding of the Meiji constitutional experience. Because of their lack of systematic knowledge concerning Western political theory, they showed an incapacity to clearly distinguish between traditional concepts of imperial authority and Western constitutional concepts of limited authority. Moreover, their knowledge of the Meiji constitution was filtered through the conservative views of Itō and Hozumi. There is no evidence that they sought the views of Japanese liberals like Ōkuma or Inukai; and even if they had, it is doubtful that they would have had an understanding of or sympathy for them.

In addition, one should note that the Meiji constitutional model was itself extremely ambiguous. As one scholar recently put it: "The Meiji political system both in theory and practice was a mixture of authoritarianism and constitutionalism, a hybrid 'absolute constitutional monarchy.' "[30] This hybrid model has stimulated both liberal and absolutist interpretations in Japanese history as well as in Western scholarship about Japan. It should not surprise us, therefore, that Liang could derive from it an essentially liberal interpretation while the Ch'ing reformers found a fulfillment of their absolutist assumptions.

In the final analysis, the impact of the Meiji model on the Ch'ing reformers and Liang was chimerical. For both, it created the illusion that because Japan had achieved strength and power under the Meiji constitutional system, China could do the same. It was an illusion soon to be dashed in 1911.

NOTES

1. For an excellent study of the difference between the radical reformers and the conservative reformers, see Hsiao Kung-ch'uan, "Weng T'ung-ho and the Reform Movement of 1898" in *Tsing Hua Journal of Chinese Studies*, Vol. I, 1957.

2. Liang Ch'i-ch'ao, "Li hsien-fa" (On establishing a constitution), in *Yin-ping-shih ho-chi* (Complete works from the ice drinker's studio; hereafter cited *"YPSHC"*; Shanghai, 1936), Vol. 2, Sec. 5, p. 6–7.

3. For a perceptive account of the Ch'ing constitutional missions, see E-tu Zen Sun, "The Chinese Constitutional Missions of 1905–06" in *Journal of Modern History*, XXIV.3:251–68 (Sept. 1952).

4. Richard C. Howard, "Japan's Role in the Reform Program of K'ang Yu-wei," in *Kang Yu-wei: A Biography and A Symposium* (Tucson, 1967), p. 285, p. 298.

5. Sun, "Chinese Constitutional Missions," p. 258.

6. *North China Herald*, August 10, 1906.

7. Tsai-tse, *K'ao-ch'a cheng-chih jih-chi* (Diary on the study of political systems; Peking, 1908), pp. 9–9b.

8. *Ibid.*, p. 13b.

9. *North China Herald*, August 10, 1906.

10. Tsai-tse, *K'ao-ch'a cheng-chih jih-chi*, p. 13b.

11. Tai Hung-tz'u and Tuan-fang, *Ou-mei cheng-chih yao-i* (The essence of European and American governments; Peking, 1907), pp. 33, 35.

12. Tsai-tse, *K'ao-ch'a cheng-chih jih-chi*, p. 22b.

13. *Ibid.*, p. 14.

14. Tai and Tuan, *Ou-mei cheng-chih yao-i*, p. 45b.

15. *Ibid.*, pp. 44–46, 49.

16. Tsai-tse, *K'ao-ch'a cheng-chih yih-chi*, p. 22b.

17. *Ibid.*, p. 9b.

18. *North China Herald*, August 5, 1910.

19. Tai and Tuan, *Ou-mei cheng-chih yao-i*, pp. 2b–5, 64–65.

20. *North China Herald*, July 15, 1910.

21. Liang Ch'i-ch'ao, "Li hsien-fa," p. 5.

22. For a detailed and thorough examination of these three articles, see

George Macklin Wilson, "Politics and the People: Liang Ch'i-ch'ao's View of Constitutional Developments in Meiji Japan Before 1890," *Papers on Japan* (Cambridge, 1961), I, 189–226. My discussion owes much to his analysis.

23. Liang Ch'i-ch'ao, "Jih-pen yu-pei li hsien shih-tai chih jen-min" (The Japanese people in the period of constitutional preparation), in *Hsin-min ts'ung pao* (New citizenry), 4.11:2–4.

24. *Ibid.*, 4.17:8–9.

25. *Ibid.*, 4.17:9–14.

26. *Ibid.*, 4.11:18.

27. Liang Ch'i-ch'ao, "Chun-chi ta-chen shu-ming yu li hsien kuo chih kuo-wu ta-chen fu-shu" (On the countersignature of the minister of army and minister of state), *YPSHC*, Vol. 9, Sec. 25a, pp. 55–56.

28. Liang Ch'i-ch'ao, "Ching-kao kuo-jen chih wu-chieh hsien-cheng che" (A warning to the people about misunderstanding constitutionalism), *YPSHC*, Vol. 10, Sec. 26, p. 62.

29. Liang Ch'i-ch'ao, "Lun chuan-chih chen-t'i yu pai hai yu chun-chu wu i li" (How despotism cannot but harm the monarch), in *Yin-ping-shih wen-chi* (Literary works of the ice-drinker's studio; Hong Kong, 1958), III, 62–73.

30. Joseph Pittau, *Political Thought in Early Meiji Japan, 1868–1889* (Cambridge, 1967), p. 201. For another study which shows the ambiguity of the Meiji constitutional development, see George Akita, *Foundations of Constitutional Government in Modern Japan* 1868–1900 (Cambridge, 1967).

The *Shishi* Interlude in Old Siam: An Aspect of the Meiji Impact in Southeast Asia[1]

E. Thadeus Flood
University of Santa Clara

In dealing with the phenomenon of Pan-Asian thinking in the Meiji period, the historian encounters almost inexhaustible materials that apparently nourish a vague conspiracy theory for Japanese political expansion.[2] The present study, which focuses on the attempt by a few Japanese activists in the 1890's to plant the seeds of Pan-Asian solidarity in the kingdom of Siam, is no exception. The similarity between the ideas of these activitists and those of the more disciplined militarists of the Shōwa era compels us to remind ourselves again of the importance of *conjoncture* and context in dealing with the history of ideas. This is all the more true in that this paper must give regrettably short shrift to considerations of *ambiance* and to the historical context to which these Meiji Pan-Asianist ideas were in fact wedded. The purpose herein is merely to discuss and evaluate one brief but instructive interlude in Meiji Japan's relations with Siam in which Japanese Pan-Asianism was put to one of its earliest and severest tests. For the wider context of late nineteenth-century Japan and Siam, the works of M. B. Jansen and D. K. Wyatt are recommended to put the present study in better perspective.[3]

The Resumption of Official Relations

In the sixteenth and seventeenth centuries, the catalyst of European presence in Japan and the emergence there of restless elements thrown up by the political, social, and economic transformations of that age encouraged a number of Japanese to migrate, some temporarily, some permanently, to the kingdom of Siam. Under a succession of community leaders, including the much-romanticized Yamada Nagamasa, these emigrants and expatriates achieved considerable economic and political power in Siam, if only for a very brief period. The exclusionist policies of the Tokugawa shogunate and Japanese involvement in domestic Siamese political intrigues led to the decline and eventual disappearance of the Japanese settlement in Siam, though it was kept alive in story and legend in Japan throughout the Tokugawa period. Formal contacts between the two states ceased, however, for a period of 241 years (1634 to 1875).[4]

Some of the same factors that in the colorful "Era of Yamada Nagamasa" impelled Japanese to venture into Siam were again operative, *mutatis mutandis,* in the late nineteenth century when a new chapter opened in Japan's relations with Siam. Again there was a European presence in Japan, accompanied by important political and socioeconomic changes that produced a frustrated warrior class and an emancipated merchant class. Once again, therefore, in the 1870's, the eighties, and the nineties, the regions of Southeast Asia, over which the Wako pirates and Red Seal trading ships of old had ranged, were rediscovered by probing Japanese. As each new and exotic tale of these tropic lands appeared in Japan, interest in the region increased.

One of the earliest examples of this Meiji genre of "South Seas" lore was Ōtori Keisuke's *Shamu Kikō* (Journey to Siam), written by the first Japanese to visit that country since the early seventeenth century.[5] Although the Ōtori mission of 1875 was not an official diplomatic embassy, Ōtori was a government official (of the old ministry of public works or *kōbushō*) and his objective was to investigate conditions in Siam and to arrange for eventual formal treaty relations with that country.[6] In interviews with Ōtori, the young king Rama V of Siam, first showed an interest that he would long maintain in Japan's response to the common problem of Western encroachment in Asia.

The Japanese did not pursue the matter of treaty relations with Siam, most probably because they themselves became engrossed in treaty revision problems with the West. Four years after the Ōtori visit, however, Siam took the initiative and through an intermediary informed the Tokyo foreign office that they were anxious to pursue the matter of treaty relations brought up by Ōtori.[7]

The full explanation for the Siamese desire in 1879 to conclude a treaty with Japan must await a study of Bangkok archives. It surely stemmed in part, at least, from the initial administrative reforms of the young Siamese monarch Rama V, which included the creation of a Western-style, independent department for foreign affairs in 1875.[8]

The Siamese interest in a treaty may also have been related to her peculiar international position. Siam was under heavy Western imperialist pressure at this juncture and was in need of diplomatic support. She could no longer look to China for this, given the latter's obvious weakness after the Opium War, and the kings of Siam had already begun to ease their country out of the traditional tributary relationship with the Middle Kingdom. China, on the other hand, had rejected Siamese requests in 1878 for a new diplomatic relationship of Western-style equality. Siamese inquiries to Japan in 1879 probably reflected the failure to institute such relations on a basis of equality with China.[9]

In response to the Siamese, Japan replied that it was preoccupied with its own treaty revision problems but that it ultimately intended to establish regular treaty relations with Siam.[10] No further contact on the official level occurred until mid-1887 when Rama V of Siam transmitted a personal request to the Meiji Emperor that diplomatic relations be resumed. He indicated his "sincere desire to bring to an end any misunderstandings" that might have existed between the two countries—a reference to events in the early seventeenth century that led to the long lapse in official relations. The same letter introduced the king's younger brother and (since 1885) minister of foreign affairs, Prince Theewawoŋ (Devawongse) as minister plenipotentiary to negotiate the resumption of relations with Japan.[11]

Prince Theewawoŋ was then abroad on a special mission to study Western political institutions; he was scheduled to return home by way of Japan.[12] He arrived in Tokyo in September 1887 and, after an audience with the Meiji emperor, he signed a "Declaration of Friendship and Commerce" with Japan's Vice-Foreign Minister Aoki Shūzō.[13]

One important factor behind this Siamese initiative of 1887 seems to have been Rama V's interest in Japan's ongoing educational reforms. This was manifest in January 1888 when another royal emissary, Cawphrajaa Phaadsakɔrawoŋ (Bhaskarawongse) journeyed to Tokyo to exchange the newly-ratified "Declaration of Friendship." Phaadsakɔrawoŋ, who was soon to become minister of education himself and who figures importantly in this study, was accompanied by an official of the Education Department, Khun Wɔrakaan Koson (Thabthim Bunjaradphan, later Phrajaa Phinidsaaraa). The latter spent the next five months in Japan at the behest of Rama V, making a study of the Japanese school system.[14] His subsequent report does not seem to have been utilized by the Siamese, however, and, in spite of the king's interest, no further steps were taken to implement the 1887 "Declaration of Friendship."

"South Seas Fever" in Japan

Although there were no noteworthy official relations between Japan and Siam between 1888 and 1897, it was in this brief period that an active Japanese interest in the latter country first manifested itself, albeit on an unofficial level. This was in turn related to the shifting emigration and colonization discussions that had been carried on in Japan continuously since the Meiji Restoration of 1868.[15]

The idea of colonization in early Meiji years was limited to the Tōhoku and the northern islands—strictly a domestic affair. The Hawaii and Guam emigration ventures were both arranged by the previous Tokugawa government and were carried out in 1868 against the orders (as in the Hawaii enterprise) or without the direct knowledge (as in the Guam affair) of the Meiji government.[16] On a number of subsequent occasions in the first decade of its existence the new government exhibited its reluctance to endorse any emigration projects abroad (other than those in the north).[17]

Despite this negative official attitude in the early Meiji period, certain individuals dreamed of more distant fields for Japanese emigration activity abroad. For analytical purposes these individuals can be singled out as exponents of a peculiar form of expansion quite distinct from the more purely political-military expansionism calling for expeditions against Korea or Taiwan.[18] A closer look at these emigration advocates will show, however, that in almost every case their projects are but variants of, and not essentially different from, the general idea of political expansion abroad. The political nuance can be found in the abstract emigration arguments of Taguchi Ukichi, who pioneered in publicizing the need for southward commercial development in Taiwan and the South Seas.[19] The same nuance can be found in the thinking of the leading emigration advocate of the Meiji era, Admiral Enomoto Takeaki. This is of particular relevance here, for Enomoto, more than any other, gave the greatest impetus to Japanese emigration and colonizing attempts in the Malay Peninsula and Siam in the 1890's. These latter in turn provided the framework in that area for several years of *minkan shishi* (non-governmental activist) activity which highlighted Japan's relations with Siam in the Meiji period.

At a time when the Meiji government was discouraging the emigration of its people to Southeast Asia, Enomoto was conducting a solitary campaign to ensure a permanent Japanese presence there. His notions were a compound of defensive concern (as an old naval man familiar with the South Seas) about the encroachments of the West in Southeast Asia and a recognition of Japan's need for a secure avenue for maritime trade with Australia and the West through the Indian Ocean. In his mind, the means by which this secure avenue could be effected was emigration and colonization—two words of roughly the same significance for many Meiji emigration enthusiasts. This conjuncture of emigration and political expansion was precisely what captured the fancy of the late-Meiji *shishi* who appeared, most often with the direct backing of Enomoto, on the Malay Peninsula and Siam in the 1890's. In advocating such things as the purchase of the Marianas ("Radorōnen" or Ladrones), and the assimilation of Guam, Papua, and the Solomons by Japan in 1876-77, Enomoto was, as his biographer aptly notes, many years ahead of his countrymen.[20]

In another fashion too, Enomoto served the cause of emigration to the maritime areas stretching southwards from the Japanese archipelago. In 1879 he and several like-minded individuals formed the Tokyo Geographic Society (Tōkyō Chigaku Kyōkai). The bulletin of this group often carried articles by proponents of maritime emigration ventures and sometimes of outright military expeditions to the south.[21] These articles constitute the beginnings of a distinctive genre of Japanese journalism and romantic prose devoted to tropical Southeast Asia. During the 1880's, the bulk of this kind of literature gradually swelled *pari passu* with new travel and exploration accounts, as the process of Japanese discovery of the South Seas continued.[22]

This progressive accumulation of lore about the maritime south heralded, and no doubt helped to bring about, a shift in emphasis towards that area of the world in the discussions in Japan on emigration and colonization.[23] By the end of the 1880's, the old erudite arguments rationalizing the resettlement of the losers in the Restoration Wars had evolved considerably. Miyake Setsurei, the Meiji publicist, could later write of the new atmosphere in these terms: "The 'colonial fever' at that time and especially the 'South Seas fever' *(Nan'yō netsu)* was very strong. Most people have forgotten this today, but it was awfully high at that time. It must have been the influence of Germany. . . . It was said in Japan that we had to acquire colonies from somewhere, and every possibility was checked."[24]

It is clear that the "South Seas fever" of which Miyake spoke was almost exclusively directed towards insular Southeast Asia. The writings and activities of such pioneers in "southern expansion" *(nanshin)* proposals as Taguchi Ukichi, Enomoto Takeaki, Yokoo Tōsaku, Suzuki Keikun, Sugiura Jugo, Suganuma Teifu, Shige Shigetaka, and others in the 1880's are oriented towards the Philippines, the Marshalls, Marianas, and Carolinas, but there is almost no attention to Japan's future role in the Malay Peninsula, Siam, and the adjacent areas of mainland Southeast Asia.[25] Japan's relations with Siam had been quiescent since the 1887 Declaration of Friendship, with the exception of one or two adventuresome merchants who set up shop in Bangkok. The situation would probably have remained thus for some time had it not been for an unusually energetic and ambitious Japanese diplomatic agent in Singapore, Saitō Miki.

Saitō was Japan's first consul stationed in Singapore, and almost immediately after his appointment there in 1890, he began to draw attention to the potential of the Malay Peninsula and Siam for Japanese emigration and colonization. By the time Admiral Enomoto Takeaki assumed the post of foreign minister in the first Matsukata Cabinet in May 1891, Saitō was already full of ideas about the future of Japan in that part of the world and the role of emigration in making that future. His plans are worth noting because they foreshadow the framework in which the *shishi* emigration movement in Siam would be carried out.

Saitō's plans are revealed in a conversation he held with ex-Foreign Minister Aoki Shūzō in Singapore in May 1892. From Saitō's *procès verbale* of this talk we learn that he advocated that Japan undertake colonization in the northern part of the Malay Peninsula (since the southern portion was already too much under British control). He noted that the northern part, roughly from the Isthmus of Kra down along the east coast to Trengganu, was entirely in Siamese territory but that it was inhabited only by savages and that Siamese sovereignty was only nominal. "If suitable areas were located and if the Siamese government were approached to recognise the emigration of our nationals . . .

it may be imagined how greatly it would aid the future expansion of our position and power in Asia." He then came to the *pièce de résistance* of his Siam emigration ideas: Japanese control of a Kra canal, to neutralize the British at Singapore and give Japan control of the maritime commerce plying between the Indian Ocean and the Far East. ". . . If perchance our nationals could emigrate to areas around the Isthmus of Kra and, after occupying this great, wild expanse of land, were to seek out at an appropriate time favorable points for controlling the Isthmus, and if they were to excavate a canal across it, well it is clear as can be that this territory of the Japanese Empire, sitting astride the canal, would mean the seizure of the commercial supremacy of the eastern and western seas."

Saitō was interested in eventual colonization of southwestern peninsular Siam by Japanese, therefore, but he envisioned this as a gradual emigration movement northwards towards the Isthmus of Kra from a base on the southwest coast. For the moment, then, he advocated preliminary emigration surveys all along the southwest coast of the Malay Peninsula from Johore northwards. Aoki Shuzō was enthusiastic, and at his suggestion Saitō wrote of his plans to the new foreign minister, Enomoto Takeaki.[26]

Enomoto, who had bombarded the government with memorials on the need for a maritime policy in the south since the mid-1870's, was, in his post as foreign minister, in an excellent position to carry out his own plans. In July 1891, over the objections of less visionary members of the Matsukata Cabinet, he set up an emigration section *(imin-ka)* attached to the cabinet secretariat *(daijin kanbō)*.[27] This was Japan's first government office set up expressly to facilitate emigration abroad. The new section, of course, needed information on suitable sites; and Enomoto, using his position as foreign minister, mobilized various Japanese consuls scattered throughout the South Seas to conduct preliminary surveys for him. He thus welcomed Saitō's ideas and endorsed his plans for the Malay Peninsula. Saitō carried out a survey of that area in 1893 and, in 1894 while on an official mission to Siam, made another survey there.[28]

It was roughly at this point that the enthusiasm for emigration enterprises and the general "South Seas fever" of the times were translated into action in Japan by a growing number of *shishi-rōnin* (activist-drifter) types who were in the traditions of Ōi Kentarō's Pan-Asianism. The encouragement of emigration schemes by such men as Enomoto and Saitō provided the opportunity for a host of Japanese adventurers, ne'er-do-wells, political malcontents and even a few daring businessmen to seek their fortunes in Siam.

The Shishi *Interlude in Siam*

The *shishi* Pan-Asian movement in Japan in the late Meiji period has already received excellent monographic treatment in English and requires no introduction here.[29] Suffice it to say that a number of remarkable representatives of this *shishi* tradition, with all the usual connections with the liberal opposition and the economic and historical ties to southwest Japan—particularly the Kumamoto area—made their debut on the Asian scene in Siam in the mid-1890's, shortly before their main appearance in the Chinese revolution. Their story in Siam is of interest not because they conquered, for they in fact failed miserably in their involute designs there, but rather because these Pan-Asian idealists confronted another independent "Asian" country possessed of an advanced culture, but one not within the Sino-Confucian civilization complex. In a sense Siam was a test case for Okakura Tenshin's thesis that Asia was "one": the very essence of Pan-Asianism.[30] Their story is important too because it adds to our cumulative knowledge of the Japanese image of Asia—an image that did not die with the *shishi* failures in Siam and later in China. Finally, their story is important because it forms a hitherto unknown aspect of Japan's relations with Siam and Southeast Asia in the Meiji era.

The first of a number of Japanese *shishi* adventurers who sought heroic destinies in Siam was one Iwamoto Chizuna, a solitary figure not at first connected with the emigration activities of Saitō Miki and Enomoto Takeaki.[31] It is significant, however, that he soon found he could best translate his own long-range altruistic schemes in Siam into action through the medium of emigration projects. The official history of the Kokuryūkai (Amur River or Black Dragon Society) dubbed him as dissolute, untamed, irascible and temperamental.[32] In his own memoirs Iwamoto confided that he was "of a careless disposition" and somewhat "impatient with details and trifles."[33] Born in 1858 the son of a samurai, his entire life was a monument to these characterizations. He was cashiered from the army in 1888 for continuing to associate with liberal opposition leaders (such as

Inukai Tsuyoshi) who were at odds with the government. He thereby joined a horde of other young activists who were deeply concerned about government repression at home and the tense Far Eastern situation abroad.

Iwamoto was too much the man of action, however, and he determined to take positive steps of his own by journeying through the lands of the Orient. By sheer chance he was encouraged to go to Siam by an old samurai from Akizuki Han whose son had been adopted in 1888 by the Siamese statesman Cawphrajaa Phaadsakɔrawoŋ when the latter visited Japan. The son, Yamamoto Yasutarō, was to be his contact in Bangkok.[34]

In August 1892, Iwamoto set out alone on a third-class booking from Kobe to Singapore with ten yen in his pocket. Utterly impoverished by the time he reached Singapore, he was able to pawn some clothing and his hat, and with the six yen proceeds he continued his journey to Bangkok, arriving there in September 1892, hatless, shoeless, dressed in a grimy Western-style suit, unable to speak any foreign language. This inauspicious arrival truly foreshadowed a decade of uninterrupted fiascos that awaited him in Siam.

On arrival in Bangkok, Iwamoto sought out Yamamoto Yasutarō. This man, together with another Japanese youth, Yamamoto Shinsuke, had been brought back to Siam in 1888 and given an extensive classical Siamese education at the royal school for nobility in Bangkok, the Suan Kulaab (Rose Garden) School —no doubt the first and perhaps the only foreigners to attend this exclusive institute.[35] Educated in the same way as upper-class Siamese youth, both were in 1892 fluent in Siamese as well as English. Very little is known of Yamamoto Shinsuke except that in 1897 he accompanied Iwamoto Chizuna on the latter's 111-day scouting journey through Siam, Laos, and Annam and as a result died in Hanoi. The other Yamamoto, Yasutarō, played a more active role in Siamese-Japanese relations; when Iwamoto arrived in Bangkok in 1892 he was working as an interpreter for the Siamese ministry of education, headed by his adopted "father," Phaadsakɔrawoŋ.[36] Through this Yamamoto, Iwamoto Chizuna was introduced to the latter and also to one of Siam's eminent military men, Minister of Agriculture Cawphrajaa Surasag. Phaadsakɔrawoŋ, in adopting the two Japanese youths in 1888, had already displayed his sympathies for Japan and would continue to do so. Surasag, a soldier and Siam's most militant nationalist of this period, soon became an even more obvious admirer of the Japanese and proved to be their greatest support in Siam.[37]

According to Iwamoto's account, it was with the support and endorsement of Phaadsakɔrawoŋ and Surasag that he returned to Japan in February 1893 to acquaint political leaders with the dangers facing Siam from the West, and the need to revise Japan's Far Eastern policies accordingly. Siam was indeed in a tense struggle with France at this time over the Laos region, but Iwamoto's attempts to persuade his countrymen of the dangers were in vain. He was viewed as an "itinerant swindler," and his warnings were received with "cold smirks" and nothing more. He finally succeeded in interesting a ministry of commerce and agriculture official in a business venture in Siam, and was in Kobe making preparations to return to that country when he heard the news of the "Franco-Siamese Incident."[38]

France had finally broken with Siam over the issue of who was to control the old Siamese vassal states of upper Laos. On July 13, 1893, French gunboats forced their way up the Chao Phraya River and threatened Bangkok in an incident that had profound repercussions not only in Siam but in Europe as well.[39] Iwamoto's reaction was typically precipitate. When he heard of the incident on July 30, 1893, he dropped everything, boarded a ship the next day, and made a dash to rescue Siam.

On his way, Iwamoto encountered in Shanghai another young Japanese itinerant adventurer who was hurrying to Siam for the same reason as himself. This was Ishibashi Usaburō, another classic representative of the late-Meiji *shishi* activists.[40] At twenty-four years of age Ishibashi had already worked as a dishwasher in San Francisco, studied politics and economics at Lincoln High School and Oakland Polytech in California, fought with a band of American volunteers in a revolutionary war in Chile, and had now returned to Asia to espouse the cause of Pan-Asianism. When he heard of the French aggression in Siam, he too made a heroic dash to Bangkok. He was stopped short in Shanghai when his funds were temporarily depleted—a commonplace condition for these men.

After talking with Iwamoto, the two evolved a plan to save Siam from the clutches of French imperialism. Ishibashi borrowed funds from another *shishi* friend and reached Siam on the next boat after Iwamoto, but they arrived just after the

Franco-Siamese peace talks had ended and Siam had already signed a humiliating treaty with France (October 3, 1893).[41]

Neither of these men was easily discouraged. With the help of the language expert Yamamoto Yasutarō, they contacted the two Japanophiles within the Siamese government, Phaadsakɔrawoŋ, minister of education, and Surasag, minister of agriculture (after 1892). To these men and anyone else who would listen they pleaded the Pan-Asian theme that Siam must not be gobbled up by the Westerners. Their solution to Siam's problems was the emigration of large numbers of Japanese into the country—apparently on the premise that Japan had already successfully resisted the Europeans and could do the same for Siam. To this end, they talked of setting up an emigration company, and even spoke of an eventual Siamese-Japanese alliance, the latter being quite in the traditions of such Asianists as Tarui Tōkichi and Suganuma Teifu.[42]

The reception in Siam of this kind of peculiarly Japanese sentiment about Asia and its future was apparently not very great. Yet there can be no doubt that at least two high-ranking Siamese nobles in positions of importance in the government lent a very sympathetic ear to these unofficial paladins of Asian solidarity. Phaadsakɔrawoŋ, minister of education, continued to provide the two Japanese with living quarters. Surasag used his influence as a prominent military man and as minister of agriculture to enable them to lease several extensive parcels of ground to serve as agricultural bases for Japanese colonization. It is difficult to locate these leased areas from Japanese descriptions because of the unsuitability of Japanese *kana* for rendering Siamese sounds and because of the arbitrary way in which the Japanese used Chinese characters for Siamese place names at this time. It seems fairly clear, however, that Surasag leased a 700-acre parcel to Iwamoto and Ishibashi in the district of Sapathum, near (at the present time within) Bangkok. Japanese sources point out—correctly—that this land was part of the royal estates of the Siamese Crown Prince (until his death in 1895) Cawfaa Wachirunnahid.[43]

Other contemporary Japanese sources specifically note leases of land from the ministry of agriculture on "special contract" (*tokuyaku*) at this same time in other areas, notably an approximately nine-square-mile lease on the east (right) bank of the Chao Phraya River in the area of Ayuthia, and another lease possibly near the mouth of the Chao Phraya River.[44] These, too, were apparently leased to Iwamoto and Ishibashi. The role of Minister of Agriculture Surasag was essential in the taking of such extensive leases by several obscure Japanese, and this is indeed one of our clearest indications that for a brief moment at the end of the nineteenth century certain members of the Siamese nobility gave some credence to the romantic, Pan-Asian message of the Meiji *shishi*.

Word of the extensive land leases by Japanese in Siam spread quickly among colonization devotees and *shishi* activists, particularly since this was the time when the "colonial fever" was at its peak in Japan. By the spring of 1894 Japanese in Shanghai were telling each other of the large plots of land acquired by their countrymen in Siam, and it was bruited about that the Japanese population there would soon top a thousand.[45]

Meanwhile, Iwamoto and Ishibashi confidently formed the Siam Colonization Society (Shamu Shokumin Kyōkai), and then set about recruiting Japanese peasants to realize their plans. Ishibashi departed for Japan while Iwamoto continued to make preparations in Bangkok. He scurried about enlisting the aid of a few wandering *shishi-rōnin* who were now beginning to appear on diverse missions. Among these latter was one Kumagai Naosuke, who drifted to Siam in late 1893, apparently on emigration scouting duties for Enomoto, judging from a letter written by him in February 1894.

Kumagai's letter well illustrates the mentality of many of the Japanese activists in the tropics at this time and is worth quoting *in extenso* for its flavor alone. Writing to a friend in Japan, Kumagai noted that he had already finished three arduous "scouting trips" in Siam's interior, and he complains of mountain crossings in the north, river fordings in the south, poisonous serpents overhead, treacherous ground underfoot, malaria, crocodiles and, with humor he adds: "If only I had had some money my trip would have made Stanley's exploration of Dark Africa not worth a poop *(hi ni arazaru koto)*."

He then recounted a trip made recently to the old capital at Ayuthia (where he leased emigration land) to visit the remains of the Japanese seventeenth-century settlement there: "I raised a wooden monument and inscribed on it in large characters: 'REMAINS OF A JAPANESE SETTLEMENT,' and on the back I inscribed: 'JANUARY 1, 1894, KUMAGAI OF GREAT JAPAN ERECTED THIS.' Then, amidst the flowers of the fields and the cool waters, I grieved for the great spirit of Yamada

Nagamasa, and just at that moment the moon came up and the whole scene carried me back to the exploits of 300 years ago; I was suddenly overcome with deep emotion."

He ended with the following appeal to his friend: ". . . the land of Siam awaits the coming of the Japanese. . . . Why not stop struggling over that little patch of earth and be the first in this heroic attempt? I've fetched some native wine from the village market and I await your coming!"[46]

Romantic, sentimental idealism of this kind was coupled with some very firm ideas on the political objectives of the *shishi* in Siam, as can be seen from the following extract from a letter written by Ishibashi Usaburō, one of the two organizers of the Siam Colonization Society. Writing to a friend in Shanghai in March 1894, Ishibashi confided that his colonization plans were moving forward and outlined the latter as follows:

> My ideas on Siam are (1) to expand the work of colonization there and to establish a latent Japanese influence; (2) to install Japanese in the Siamese government; (3) to purchase all Siamese railroad stock; (4) to purchase the Malay Peninsula. While this might appear unkind in regard to Siam, our objective is to compete with the white man in Central Asia and hence does not affect the welfare of the Orient in the least. Thus we expect to put the above four steps into effect.[47]

In Japan, Ishibashi had now made contact with Enomoto Takeaki and a number of other emigration enthusiasts, but his arrangements for a group of emigrants for Siam were delayed time after time. In Bangkok, Iwamoto, the man of action, could stand idle no longer and hurried back to Japan himself to take matters in hand. By December 1894, he succeeded in gathering about thirty colonists together with the aid of Enomoto Takeaki, and departed with them for Siam via Hong Kong.[48] With his distaste for pecuniary details, he had neglected to secure sufficient funds for himself and his charges to get to Siam. He sailed from Kobe with only nine yen left after purchasing fares as far as Hong Kong. As he later put it, he relied on getting the rest of the money "some way or other" in Hong Kong, and, if this were not possible, he was prepared to "battle tooth and nail" to see that the colonists got through. Despite this resolution, he found himself stranded in the old *"Tōyō Ryokan"* (Oriental Inn)—a famous inn catering to China *rōnin* in Hong Kong—in March

1895. He was destitute and had thirty hungry, bewildered Japanese peasants on his hands.[49]

Iwamoto's negligence, which was typical of so many of the ill-starred emigration ventures of the time, might have meant an end to the Siam Colonization Society's plans had it not been for the arrival of the Siamese minister of agriculture, Surasag, in Hong Kong just at that moment. His unexpected appearance there while on his way to Japan with his protégé, Yamamoto Yasutarō, enabled Iwamoto to impose upon him for funds to continue the journey, and the first group of Japanese emigrants to Siam finally reached their destination safely.[50]

The Siam Colonization Society was now reorganized into a commercial firm, the Siam Colonization Company (Shamu Shokumin Kaisha), and a host of young Japanese activists, wandering *rōnin,* and self-styled heirs of the samurai tradition were installed on the payroll in various managerial capacities. No president was named (perhaps Surasag was slated for this post), but Iwamoto became vice-president, with Ishibashi (just returned) and Yamamoto Yasutarō as company directors. The scouting enthusiast Kumagai Naosuke became company "advisor," and two other young firebrands, Arakawa Gagoro and Matsuno Yasutarō, were named "company secretary" and "supervisor of emigration" respectively.[51]

This was the apogee in the brief history of the Siam Colonization Company. The ebullient Iwamoto Chizuna was especially confident (even arrogant, some said) in April 1895 as he departed for Japan again, announcing that he would return this time with over a hundred emigrants. His spirits were bolstered too by the fact that he carried with him "several thousand yen" in funds borrowed from Minister of Agriculture Surasag to finance recruiting operations, and several hundred yen in "earnest money" from a Japanese firm in Bangkok desirous of hiring workers in Japan. To further enhance his euphoric state of mind, he was carrying a Siamese sword fashioned from gold, a treasured family heirloom entrusted to him by Surasag in the hope that he could have it polished and repaired in Japan.[52] Little wonder then that Surasag and the staff of the Siam Colonization Company grew increasingly annoyed as the months passed and nothing was heard from Iwamoto.

Surasag gave unstinting aid to the company's efforts in Siam, providing Siamese workers to help the farmers prepare their plots for sowing, for the latter were completely unfamiliar with tropical soils and cultivation techniques. The seed was about to be sown when the Japanese emigrants suddenly stopped working *en masse* and demanded that the company advance them their loan, "as per the contract." The managers were dumbfounded, never having heard of any sort of arrangements for loans, or indeed of any contract. They were furious when they learned that Iwamoto, in his zeal to attract colonists, had written and signed such a contract with the latter, stipulating, among other things, that each settler could have an advance of 50 yen from the company upon arriving in Siam, to be paid back after the harvest in monthly installments. Iwamoto, with his characteristic distaste for "trivia," had failed to mention the contract to his compatriots and instead had hurried off to Japan armed with most of the company's funds, leaving his compatriots to fend for themselves.[53]

With the farmers now refusing to labor in the fields until they received their promised advance, Ishibashi was forced to turn to the company's old benefactor, Surasag. This noble gentleman had already funded Iwamoto's and Ishibashi's several trips to and from Japan, the emigrants' fares from Hong Kong, the expense of leasing and developing the settlement area—in short he was the principal financial factor behind the entire colonization enterprise in Siam. The chronic impoverishment and mismanagement of the *shishi* were apparently straining his purse, if not his moral commitment to Pan-Asianism, and he adamantly refused to rescue the company from this quandary.[54]

By May 1895 the colonists, facing imminent starvation, were beset with unexpected danger from another quarter. In that month several "unscrupulous" Japanese then in Bangkok approached the group and recruited a few to work as coolies on the railroads then under construction in the Korat area of the northeast. Nothing more was heard of these unfortunates, and they were presumably casualties in that early "railroad of death" project which reportedly killed some forty Japanese and some three hundred Chinese laborers, mostly because of the malarial conditions there.

In the same month the dwindling emigrant group was approached by recruiters from a French mining concern in southwestern Siam. Since they had few alternatives, fifteen of the Japanese farmers were induced to work in the mines. By September 1895, four of the original fifteen came straggling back to Bangkok, emaciated and sick, pleading for help. They reported that their fellow laborers were either already dead or dying at the mines. Though the *shishi* managers had tried to warn the emigrants of the dangers in working in the mines, this report nevertheless stirred their samurai instincts. After committing the survivors to a hospital, Ishibashi, Arakawa, and Matsuno set out on the road south for the French mines, presumably bent on settling accounts. They did not get far before they too fell prey to the dangers of the tropics. Two became ill with jungle fever, and the three only succeeded in making it back to Bangkok through the generous aid of a tribal chieftain who rescued them on the road. A further report from the French mines indicated that there were no survivors there. To complete this growing litany of tragedies, the *shishi* were shocked to find upon their return to Bangkok that those emigrants who had not gone to work on the railroads or at the mines had now scattered, some becoming coolies, some domestic servants, all of them swallowed up in the unfamiliar world of tropical Siam. Not one remained with the company.

After this chain of fiascos which left their emigrant charges dead, diseased, or missing (though it was typical of these ventures that the *shishi* were relatively unscathed), the company managers decided to dissolve the firm. With the (presumably enthusiastic) approval of its benefactor, Cawphrajaa Surasag, the casualty-ridden career of the Siam Colonization Company ended in October 1895.[55]

The final chapter in the history of the Siam emigration movement featured a change in *dramatis personae* but did not offer relief from the tragicomic series of fiascos that haunted the *shishi* planners.

By the time Iwamoto, ebullient and well funded, arrived back in Japan in March 1895, the "colonial fever" of which Miyake Setsurei wrote was at its height. Emigration was no longer a novelty, for sizable groups of Japanese laborers and farmers had already by 1895 gone to such faraway places as Hawaii, New Caledonia, the Fijis, Guadeloupe Island, Australia, India, Canada, America, and Guatemala.[56] Not all of these ventures were successful, however, owing to the great number of ephemeral emigration firms that had been hastily formed, often by unqualified persons such as innkeepers, drifters or, as in the case of the Siam Colonization Company, visionaries with little concern for detail. A number of emigration disasters had already come to the attention of the Japanese public and were even discussed in the Diet. As a result the government in April 1894 had issued the Emigrant Protection Regulations (Imin Hogo Kisoku) in an effort to curb questionable ventures.[57]

Not surprisingly, one of the first of the undesirable promoters to be prohibited from engaging in emigration affairs was Iwamoto Chizuna, who had returned to Japan for precisely that purpose. He attempted to circumvent the regulations by scheming with some Kobe businessmen to start a company but the government refused to license it, as one chronicler suggests, "perhaps because they lacked faith in its ability to endure."[58] Iwamoto finally had to ask a legitimate firm, the Hiroshima Emigration Company (Hiroshima Imin Kaisha) to recruit emigrants for him, and they soon had about a hundred men. At this point Iwamoto himself fell seriously ill—possibly because the news of the fate of the Siam emigrants in the "French Mines Affair" was becoming public knowledge in Japan, and he was thus condemned on all sides for his cavalier conduct.

Since returning to Japan, Iwamoto's Pan-Asianist declamations on the need for Japanese "guidance-tutelage" (*keirin*) in Siam had caught the attention of youthful idealists who were casting about for some righteous cause abroad upon which to expend their energies. One of these was Miyazaki Torazō (Tōten).[59] His primary interest was in China, but he was attracted to Siam by Iwamoto's tales of the powerful overseas Chinese minority there. He saw in Siam and its overseas Chinese population an opportunity to infiltrate China "by the back door," as it were, and also to study the Chinese language and perhaps contribute to the Pan-Asianist reform and strengthening of Siam as well. Originally he planned to accompany Iwamoto and his emigrants to Siam, but, when he heard of Iwamoto's illness, he determined to go alone and visited Iwamoto to bid farewell. Iwamoto, because of his illness and perhaps fearing his own reception in Siam, made an emotional appeal to Miyazaki to take his place at the head of the emigrants and through the Siam Colonization Company (he was unaware it was defunct) to lay the basis for a Japanese colony there. Stirred by this sickbed rhetoric, Miyazaki overcame certain doubts he had previously harbored about Iwamoto's deportment and agreed to become the representative of the Hiroshima Emigration Company. After all the delays, most of the recruits had elected to go to Hawaii, and Miyazaki departed for Bangkok on October 5, 1895, with some twenty farmers.

His arrival in Bangkok in late October 1895 came some

seven months after Iwamoto had departed and only a few days after the Siam Colonization Company had come to an inglorious end. Miyazaki was taken aback, therefore, when he presented a letter of introduction from Iwamoto to Ishibashi Usaburō, and received in reply a barrage of invective aimed at the errant vice-president of the defunct company. He was told of Iwamoto's cavalier disregard for commitments, the breach-of-contract payments that had to be made, the Japanese loss of esteem among the Siamese, even including Cawphrajaa Surasag, and the consequent dissolution of the company.

Surasag had not completely abandoned the Japanese, for they were at that time quartered in one of his former residences on a tributary of the Chao Phraya River—a building large enough to house a thousand men, as Miyazaki described it. With the help of Ishibashi (who left Siam shortly thereafter) temporary employment was found for most of them in Japanese shops then operating in the Siamese capital city.[60] Miyazaki concerned himself with their welfare, acting as their interpreter and "supervisor," but he also found time to scout for further emigration possibilities in Siam. In this connection he, too, soon made the acquaintance of Siam's foremost military campaigner, Japanophile, and reluctant minister of agriculture, Cawphrajaa Surasag.

Miyazaki's impressions of this Siamese soldier-statesman vividly confirm the picture of him, available in his own memoirs and in Siamese biographies, as an unusually militant patriot. He paints Surasag as a dynamic individual, actively in sympathy with the fraternal, anticolonial, and Pan-Asianist sentiments of the Japanese *shishi* types in Siam. He rightly perceived that Surasag was bitter at having to serve in the unmilitary post of agriculture minister, and he also sympathized with the latter's discouragement at his countrymen's lack of militancy in confronting the Western threat. Miyazaki was no doubt correct in asserting that it was this very absence of any militant reaction on the part of the Siamese to the Western threat that had brought Cawphrajaa Surasag enthusiastically to encourage Japanese colonization in hopes of eventually revitalizing his own countrymen.

Surasag continued to give extraordinary and unwavering support to the Japanese *shishi* movement in Siam, even after the failure of the Siam Colonization Company. When Miyazaki called upon him in November or December 1895, he received a warm welcome. Surasag told of his admiration for Japan's advances in the world (a reference to Japan's victory in the Sino-

Japanese War, perhaps) and also told of his discouragement with his own country's situation. He questioned Miyazaki on Japan's ultimate intentions in "protecting" Korea from China in the recent war. The latter's replies are not recorded, but he apparently reassured the Siamese noble, for Surasag unhesitatingly endorsed further Japanese emigration into Siam, though he indicated he could no longer support the operation financially. "Honest officials are always poor," he told Miyazaki, but he agreed to help all he could in other ways.[61]

Miyazaki, impressed by Surasag's sincerity, resolved to persuade the Hiroshima Emigration Company to support further operations in Siam, and, after warning his emigrant charges not to be seduced by high-wage offers of employment on the Korat railway, he departed for Japan.

The Hiroshima Emigration Company rejected Miyazaki's ideas on further operations in Siam, but, despite this setback, he headed there again in March 1896 in the company of several other like-minded *shishi* who were convinced of the future possibilities of colonization projects there.[62] These hopes were severely jarred when, after a harrowing journey via Hong Kong, Swatow, and Singapore, the *shishi* arrived in Bangkok only to find that seventeen out of the original twenty emigrants Miyazaki had led to Siam earlier were now lying in the old company headquarters, suffering from cholera and malaria. They had disregarded his warnings and had been lured away by "unscrupulous" Japanese in Bangkok to work on the railroad project in the northeast.

There then followed a nightmarish climax to the Siam emigration movement. The most gravely ill peasants were placed in hospitals, and the *shishi* set themselves to care for the others in the company's headquarters in Surasag's former residence. Death was in the air, however, and after three days one of Miyazaki's own *shishi* comrades succumbed to the fever. Subsequently, six of the Japanese emigrants died in the company office, and to compound the imbroglio, even Miyazaki and the other *shishi* were desperately ill for a time.

The fact that after this experience the *shishi* were not utterly disillusioned with the future of Japanese colonization in Siam is evidence of the heroic perseverance of these activists. One suspects, nonetheless, that it was, as Miyazaki's memoirs indicate, more out of a sense of obligation for the faithful support of Cawphrajaa Surasag than out of faith in their ideas that the *shishi* agreed to make one last attempt to cultivate a crop and harvest it, just to demonstrate that all the financial expenditure and effort to date had not been in vain. They were taking no chances with the farmers, however, and resolved to rely on them no more. They would work the fields themselves. Yet even in this last gesture, they were obliged to call once again on Surasag to provide them with implements to do the job. Such was this unusual nobleman's unflagging faith in the Japanese that he even agreed to furnish them with Siamese peasants to work the land. They declined this latter offer, perhaps somewhat hastily, for these heirs of the aristocratic samurai were quite lacking in agrarian skills. Inevitably, their crops failed and, finally disconsolate, the *shishi* drifted back to Japan in the late summer of 1896, eventually to move on to more fertile fields for their bravado in China.[63] A few solitary activists appeared in Siam in subsequent years on diverse, arcane missions, but the thrust of the *shishi*-led Siam colonization movement ended on this inglorious note, and the *shishi* interlude in Siam was over.[64]

It is the private, non-governmental *shishi* activities in Siam that alone lend a certain character and historical interest to the relations between that country and Japan in the Meiji era. There were, of course, exchanges on other levels, including the governmental, in this era, but they were for the most part desultory, and were not pursued with much enthusiasm by either side. Thus, in the field of education, there were some indications in the 1880's and 1890's of an apparent Siamese interest in Japanese progress, as Professor Wyatt's researches in the Bangkok archives have recently shown.[65] Such information as the Siamese did gather on Japanese education was apparently never acted upon, however. The several Japanese "advisors" who came to Bangkok after 1892 at the request of the Japanophile Minister of Education Cawphrajaa Phaadsakɔrawoŋ were far outnumbered by European advisors and, with the possible exception of the (much later) prominent woman educator Yasui Tetsuko (who was principal of the Raachanii School, 1903 to 1906), clearly made little impact on the Siamese educational system.[66]

In the field of legal institutions, as elsewhere, the Western influence predominated. Even the legal expert, Masao Tōkichi, who was sent in 1897 by the Tokyo foreign office to assist in the revision of Siam's legal codes, was trained at the Yale School of

Law. He remained in Bangkok for sixteen years as a legal advisor to the government and, though his specific influence is difficult to assess, he was probably the most respected Japanese ever to serve in an advisory capacity in Siam. He became Japanese minister to Siam in 1920 and died there in 1921.[67]

Exchanges in the economic sphere were similarly unimposing, and whatever progress or experience Japan had accumulated by late Meiji times in this regard excited no curiosity in Siam. Only the old campaigner and Japanophile, Minister of Agriculture Cawphrajaa Surasag, consistent in his admiration for things Japanese, was active in this respect. He invited about ten sericulture experts from Japan in 1903, but their experiments in the Korat region failed, and the last one returned to Japan in 1913, shortly after Surasag left the ministry.[68]

The record of official political-diplomatic exchanges between the two states in this period was similarly unspectacular, and the details of this are in any case beyond the scope of the present paper. Suffice it to note here that the brunt of the negotiations for a regular treaty (to replace the 1887 Declaration of Friendship) was borne on the Japanese side by two officials who were conspicuous for their Pan-Asianist sentiments: Saitō Miki (discussed earlier in this paper) and Inagaki Manjirō.[69] The latter, in particular, had lengthy pre-treaty talks in Bangkok with the Siamese negotiator, Foreign Minister (Prince) Theewawoŋ, in which such sentiments emerged.[70] There is reason to think that Theewawoŋ was utterly unimpressed by this kind of talk. In any case, Inagaki's orders from Tokyo to extract from the Siamese consular jurisdiction and other "unequal" privileges enjoyed by the Western powers there quite undercut the Pan-Asian rhetoric he used.[71] With the signing at Bangkok of the Treaty of Friendship, Commerce, and Navigation on February 25, 1898, Siam was saddled with another unequal treaty, and it had little reason to consider the Japanese as any different from the Western powers, despite Inagaki's appeals in this regard.[72] Accordingly, since the two states appeared to lack any abiding mutual interests at this juncture in their histories, relations between them lapsed thereafter into an unspectacular torpor that would continue undisturbed until the repercussions of World War I began to transform the Far East.

In view of this absence of any mutual vital concerns or tangible interests between the two states, it is primarily the *shishi* interlude, as discussed in this paper, that draws the attention of the historian. In this regard the outstanding issue was, of course, the Japanese gospel of Pan-Asianism, and the always-fascinating question of to what extent it was applicable or acceptable outside of Japan—in this case in the very foreign soil of Siam. It would appear that the conspicuous roles of Cawphrajaa Phaadsakɔrawoŋ and Cawphrajaa Surasag were the exceptions here that prove the rule. The very frequency with which they are mentioned in the Japanese sources, to the utter exclusion of other Siamese, shows how narrow was the Japanese base of support and acceptance in that country. Obviously Pan-Asianism and anti-Westernism, as preached by Iwamoto, Ishibashi, and Miyazaki, did not greatly excite the Siamese, even in the dangers in the 1890's.

There are a number of possible reasons for the failure of Pan-Asianism to evoke a response in Siam, many of them intangible, such as cultural, religious, and linguistic differences and the like. It seems safe to infer, however, that a principal one was the fact that the Western presence in Siam was never extensive or obtrusive enough to generate the kind of resentment that led to a limited acceptance of romantic Pan-Asianism by certain South Chinese and Annamese anti-Western activists such as Sun Yat-sen and Phan Boi Chau. The attitude of Surasag, however, who was more familiar with the bitter side of (French) colonialism than most of his countrymen, provides a hint of how the Siamese might have responded to the *shishi* missionaries had their land indeed been colonized. Siam was not colonized by the West, however, and accordingly the heroic *shishi* interlude there was a futile exercise, *"acribus initiis, ut ferme talia, incuriosa fine."*

NOTES

1. The transliteration of Thai words herein generally follows Mary Haas, *Thai-English Student's Dictionary* (Stanford, 1964).

2. On the term "Pan-Asianism" see Hirano Yoshitarō, *Dai-Ajiashugi no rekishiteki kiso* (Historical basis of great Asianism; Tokyo, 1945), esp. pp. 1–133.

3. Marius Jansen, *The Japanese and Sun Yat-sen* (Cambridge, 1954); David Wyatt, *The Politics of Reform in Thailand* (New Haven, 1969).

4. On seventeenth-century Siamese-Japanese relations see Iwao Seiichi, *Nan'yō Nihonmachi no kenkyū* (Studies on the Japanese settlements in the

South Seas), rev. ed. (Tokyo, 1966), and Gunji Kiichi, *Jū-nana seiki ni okeru Nittai kankei* (Japan-Thai relations in the seventeenth century; Tokyo, 1943).

5. I have been unable to locate a copy of this rare book. It has been quoted extensively in Kuruma Takudō, comp., *Nankoku junreiki* (Record of a pilgrimage to the southern countries; Tokyo, 1916), pp. 130–32. On Ōtori Keisuke see Nakajima Masao, ed., *Taishi kaikoroku* (Reminiscences on China; Tokyo, 1936), II, 689 ff.; Heibonsha, ed., *Shinsen daijinmei jiten* (Newly selected biographical dictionary; Tokyo, 1937), I, 566–67.

6. This point I infer from Gaimushō kiroku (Foreign office records; hereafter cited "*GK*"), "Nissen Shūkō Tsūshō Kōkai Jōyaku teiketsu ikken" (Re the signing of the Japan-Siam Treaty of Friendship, Commerce, and Navigation), File No. 2-5-1, No. 17, letter Shinagawa (Shanghai consul) to Inoue (foreign minister), Jan. 20, 1880. Some material in this file is reproduced in Gaimushō, ed., *Nihon gaikō bunsho* (Diplomatic papers of Japan; Tokyo, 1936–), Vols. 13, 20, 29, and 30.

7. See Shinagawa to Inoue letter cited.

8. Sala Siwarag, *Nag kaanthuud Thaj* (Thai diplomats; Bangkok, 1962), esp. pp. 7–9; and Somded Kromphrajaa Damroŋ Raachaanuphaab, "Lagsana kaanpogkrɔɔŋ pratheed Thaj tɛɛ boraan" (Outline of the administration of Thailand in ancient times; Bangkok, 1955), p. 27.

9. In 1852 a Siamese tribute mission to Peking was attacked by bandits in South China and proved to be the last sent. In 1862, in reply to China's inquiries, Siam said it would resume the tribute whenever China could quell internal disorder (connected with the T'aip'ing Rebellion). In response to further Chinese inquiries in 1863 Siam's Rama IV decided to temporize, since he was not yet convinced of China's helplessness, and the final decision was left to the next reign. In 1869 the Siamese regent sent a mission to Peking asking that the tribute custom be abolished and that relations be on a basis of equality (Western style), but China refused. In 1878 a Chinese emissary, Tseng Chi-tse, passed through Siam and again insisted that Siam send tribute as of old. Siam countered with a request for a commercial treaty of equality, saying it would not send envoys under any other circumstances. China rejected this, and the next year Siam pressed the matter of treaty relations with Japan. See Hsieh Yu-jung, *Hsien-lo kuo-chih* (Siam gazetteer), rev. ed. (Bangkok, 1953), p. 61; Chadin Flood, tr., *The Dynastic Chronicles, Bangkok Era, The Fourth Reign* (Tokyo, 1965–66), I, 86 ff, II, 280–84, 300–04, III, 61–63, 151–53; G. W. Skinner, *Chinese Society in Thailand* (Ithaca, 1962), pp. 1–26.

10. See memo, Inoue to Sanjō Sanetomi, March 17, 1880, in *Nihon Gaikō Bunsho*, Vol. 13, p. 330.

11. *GK*, File 2-5-1, No. 17, Chulalonkorn to His Majesty Mutsuhito, Emperor of Japan, May 5, 1887 (English translation: original not in files). On Prince Theewawoŋ see "Sawwanid" (pseud.), "Phranaam Cawfaa, Phraoŋcaw, Mɔmjaw" (Royal names of Cawfaa, Phraoŋcaw, and Mɔmjaw; Bangkok, 1962), pp. 74–75. On the seventeenth-century break, see Iwao Seiichi, "Taijin no tai-Nichi kokkō bōeki fukkatsu undō" (Thai movement to revive state trade relations with Japan), *Tōa Bonsō* (Collected treatises on East Asia), IV, 80–122 (1941); Caraən Chajchana, *Prawadsaad Thaj* (Thai history; Bangkok, 1954), pp. 310 ff.

12. Somded Kromphraya Damroŋraachaanuphaab, *Theesaaphibaan* (Provin-

cial viceroys; Bangkok, 1960), p. 4; Pensri Duke, *Relations entre la France et la Thailande* (Bangkok, 1962, p. 104; Siwarag, *Nag kaanthuud Thaj*, pp. 1–2; Wyatt, *Politics of Reform*, p. 91.

13. Texts in *Nihon gaikō bunsho*, XX, 183–88, *British and Foreign State Papers*, LXXIX, 319–20 (1887–88). See also Thawad Raddhanaaphichaad, "Samphanthaphaab rawaaŋ Thaj kab Jiipun" (Bonds of friendship between Thailand and Japan; Bangkok, 1961), p. 165.

14. I differ from Wyatt, *Politics of Reform*, pp. 137–38, on the dates for Khun Wɔrakaan's sojourn in Japan and follow the latter's brief biography in Phrajaa Phinidsaaraa, "Nansyy hitoopathed kham khlooŋ" (The Hitōphathēd in verse; Bangkok, 1935), pp. ii–iii. For biographical data on Phaadsakɔrawoŋ, see Prajuun Phidsanaka, *Haa-sib Cawphrajaa* (Fifty Cawphrajaa; Bangkok, 1962), pp. 124–35; Wyatt, *Politics of Reform*, pp. 145 ff; Gaimushō, ed., *Gaikō nenpyō narabi ni shuyō bunsho* (Chronology and key documents on Japanese diplomacy; Tokyo, 1955), I, 102 (notes his sojourn in Japan).

15. For the following discussion I have relied heavily on the analysis of Kuroda Ken'ichi, *Nihon shokumin shisō shi* (History of Japanese colonial thought; Tokyo, 1942), esp. pp. 181–251.

16. Irie Toraji, *Hōjin kaigai hatten shi* (History of Japanese diffusion abroad; Tokyo, 1938), I, 9–25; Irie Toraji, *Meiji nanshin shikō* (Draft history of the Meiji southern advance; Tokyo, 1943), pp. 10–17.

17. Details in Irie, *Nanshin*, pp. 21–30.

18. Purely political-military expansionists would include such men as Saigō Takamori and Fukushima Jūshin. See Matsushita Yoshio, *Meiji gunsei shiron* (Historical treatise on the Meiji military system; Tokyo, 1956), I, 449 and note 1.

19. Kuroda, *Shokumin Shisōshi*, pp. 211 ff.

20. Kamo Giichi, *Enomoto Takeaki* (Tokyo, 1960), p. 239; *Dai Nihon gaikō bunsho*, IX, 365–93; Enomoto Takeaki, *Shiberiya nikki* (Siberian journal; Darien, 1939), pp. 11–12; Irie, *Nanshin*, p. 36; Gō Ryū, *Nan'yō bōeki gojū-nen shi* (A history of fifty years of South Seas trade; Tokyo, 1942), p. 179.

21. For example, the ninth number (1880) of the society's bulletin carried an article by one Sasaki Mōhō, proposing that Japan should seize New Guinea. Noted in Irie, *Nanshin*, pp. 39 ff.

22. Irie, *Nanshin*, pp. 38–40. For a bird's eye view of this increase in South Seas literature see Nihon Takushoku Kyōkai, ed., *Zōho nanpō bunken mokuroku* (Revised and enlarged bibliography on southern regions literature; Tokyo, 1943).

23. Kuroda, *Shokumin shisōshi*, pp. 239 ff.

24. Miyake Setsurei, *Yorioka Shōzō den*, quoted in Irie, *Nanshin*, pp. 116–17.

25. For Yokoo, see Irie, *Nanshin*, pp. 73–77, and J. M. Saniel, "Four Japanese in the Philippines," *Journal of Southeast Asian History*, IV.2: 1–11 (Sept., 1963). On Suzuki Keikun and the Marshall Islands surveys of 1884, see Suzuki Keikun, *Nan'yō tanken jikki* (Journal of South Seas exploration; Tokyo, 1892), esp. p. 15; Yanaibara Tadao, *Nan'yō Guntō no kenkyū* (Research on the South Seas Islands; Tokyo, 1935), pp. 39–40; Gō Ryū, *Nan'yo boeki*, pp. 174–76. On Sugiura, see Irie, *Nanshin*, pp. 77–82; Saniel, "Four Japanese," pp. 1–11. On Suganuma, see *ibid.*; Irie, *Nanshin*, pp. 81–93; Itō Kan'ichi, ed., *Nanshin Nihon no senkakushatachi* (Japanese pioneers in the southern advance;

The Shishi Interlude in Old Siam

Tokyo, 1941), pp. 193–223, and Kuroda, *Shokumin shisōshi*, pp. 24–42. On Shige, see Irie, *Nanshin*, pp. 65–73; Gō Ryū, *Nan'yō bōeki*, pp. 179–83. Biographies of all these South Seas enthusiasts are available in *Shinsen daijinmei jiten* and Nakajima, *Taishi Kaikōroku*, II.

26. Quotes from Irie, *Hattenshi*, I, 192–94.
27. Irie, *Nanshin*, pp. 111–12.
28. Irie, *Hattenshi*, I, 195; Irie, *Nanshin*, pp. 113, 118.
29. Jansen, *The Japanese and Sun Yat-sen*, passim.
30. On Okakura, see Marlene Mayo, "Attitudes toward Asia and the Beginnings of Japanese Empire," *Imperial Japan and Asia, A Reassessment*, comp. Grant Goodman (New York, 1967), pp. 20 ff.
31. Iwamoto Chizuna, *Shamu, Rōka, Annan, sankoku tanken jikki* (A journal of exploration in Siam, Laos and Annam; Tokyo, 1897), is an autobiographical work; Kuzuu Yoshihisa, *Tōa senkaku shishi kiden* (Biographies of East Asian pioneer activists; Tokyo, 1936), II, 827 and III, 29–31 ("Retsuden" section); *Shinsen daijinmei jiten*, I, 386.
32. Kuzuu, *Tōa senkaku*, II, 827.
33. Iwamoto, *Jikki*, pp. 1–2.
34. Anon., "Yamamoto Yasutarō den," Taikoku Nihonjin Kai, ed., *Sōritsu go-jū shūnen kaihō kinengo* (Association bulletin fiftieth anniversary commemorative number; Bangkok, 1963), p. 60.
35. On Yamamoto Yasutarō see "Yamamoto Yasutarō den," *passim*. The only extended mention of Yamamoto Shinsuke comes in Iwamoto, *Jikki, passim*. See note 64 below.
36. Yamamoto Yasutarō's career, like Iwamoto's was marked by a number of tragedies, usually hardest on those around him. In 1892 he was suspected of carelessness in the drowning death of a Siamese artist en route back to Siam in his charge. Sometime later he bought a steamship and went into the trading business in Siam, but the ship eventually blew up, killing the entire crew. In the late 1890's he became interpreter in the Siamese legation in Tokyo. Yamamoto finally drifted into revolutionary work in South China's Yunnan Province, where he dropped from sight in 1916. "Yamamoto Yasutarō den," *passim*.
37. See Surasag's autobiographical account: Cawphrajaa Surasagmontrii, Prawadkaan khɔɔŋ Cɔɔmphon Cawphrajaa Surasagmontrii (Chronicles of Field Marshal Cawphrajaa Surasagmontrii), 4 vols. (Bangkok, 1962). See also Phidsanaka, *Haa-sib Cawphrajaa*, pp. 208 ff., and Siiphanom Sinthɔɔŋ, "Sib-sɔɔŋ Cɔɔmphon Thaj" (Twelve Thai field marshals; Bangkok, 1963), pp. 671 ff. None of these sources mentions his interest in the Japanese at this time.
38. Quotes translated from Iwamoto, *Jikki*, p. 3.
39. On the July 13, 1893 "Franco-Siamese Crisis," see Henry Norman, *The Peoples and Politics of the Far East* (New York, 1895), Chap. XXIX; Duke, *Relations entre la France et la Thailande*, pp. 143 ff; Capitaine Seauve, *Les Relations de la France et du Siam* (Paris, 1907), pp. 53 ff; Le Boulanger, *Histoire du Laos francaise* (Paris, 1931), pp. 251 ff; W. L. Langer, *The Diplomacy of Imperialism*, 2nd ed. (New York, 1965), pp. 43 ff.
40. For background on Ishibashi see Kuzuu, *Tōa senkaku*, III, 47–48; *Shinsen daijinmei jiten*, I, 233; Irie, *Hattenshi*, I, 213–31 and II, 347–49.
41. Kuzuu, *Tōa senkaku*, II, 828 and III, 47.
42. Tarui Tōkichi, *Daitō gōhō ron* (For the great East uniting with Japan; Tokyo, 1885), esp. p. 140 concerning an "Asian Coalition" and joint Siamese-

Burmese defense of the Malay Peninsula. See Kuroda, *Shokumin shisōshi*, pp. 240–42, quoting Suganuma Teifu's *Dai Nihon shōgyōshi* (Commercial history of Great Japan) on the need for a China-Korea-Siam coalition headed by Japan.

43. "Yamamoto Yasutarō den," pp. 62–63, gives the size of the lease as 300 *chō*, which is close to the figure of 250 hectares given in Irie, *Hattenshi*, I, 213. Both these sources locate the seven-hundred-acre lease in the Sapathum area. Kuzuu, *Tōa senkaku*, III, 48 ("Retsuden") speaks of a lease in the Saladang area acquired through the good offices of Phaadsakorawoŋ and Surasag. Surasag's mansion was located in Saladang.

44. Kumagai letter, Feb. 3, 1894, in Irie, *Hattenshi*, I, 195–96.

45. Agawa, *Shamu ōkoku* (Kingdom of Siam; Tokyo, 1898), preface, notes that he first went to Siam on the strength of such rumors in June, 1894. He operated a business there for several years after that.

46. Quotations from Irie, *Hattenshi*, I, 195–96. On Kumagai (Tsuda Naosuke) see Nakajima, *Taishi kaikōroku*, II, 712, and *Shinsen daijinmei jiten*, II, 449.

47. Kuzuu, *Tōa senkaku*, III, 47–48.

48. Iwamoto, *Jikki*, p. 4; Irie, *Hattenshi*, I, 214–15; "Yamamoto Yasutarō den," p. 62.

49. Quotes from Iwamoto, *Jikki*, pp. 4–5; "Yamamoto Yasutarō den," p. 61.

50. "Yamamoto Yasutarō den," p. 62.

51. Irie, *Hattenshi*, I, 215.

52. Iwamoto, *Jikki*, pp. 4–5; Irie, *Hattenshi*, I, 215–16; "Yamamoto Yasutarō den," p. 63.

53. Irie, *Hattenshi*, I, 215–17 including a text of the contract. Iwamoto's own work, *Jikki*, naturally omits these details.

54. Irie, *Hattenshi*, I, 218–20. Surasag's refusal to further support the Japanese financially reflected his own deep indebtedness to his government. At the time of the Franco-Siamese crisis of 1893 he had recalled to service a force of five hundred veterans of his earlier campaigns against the Haw rebels in the north, although this move had no support from anyone else in the government with the possible exception of the King. Surasag outfitted, fed, paid and drilled these troops on funds he "borrowed" without authorization from his ministry of agriculture account, trusting that the ministry of defense would later reward him for these martial services. It did not, and he was left with the bill, which he was in the process of trying to settle at this time (1895). See his own account in *Prawadkaan*, IV, 278–97.

55. Irie, *Hattenshi*, I, 220–22; "Yamamoto Yasutarō den," pp. 61–62.

56. See Irie, *Hattenshi*, I, 101–20, and II, ". . . Nenpyō." According to foreign office figures there were 2,226 Japanese emigrants abroad in 1885 and 12,016 abroad by 1895. Tōgō Minoru, *Nihon shokumin ron*, pp. 257–58.

57. Text of the Imin Hogo Kisoku in Irie, *Hattenshi*, I, 114; discussed in Tōgō, *Nihon shokumin ron*, pp. 254–55. There were thirty-six legitimate emigration companies operating by 1903: Tōgō, pp. 276–79 (names). Of these, two had operated earlier in Siam or the Malay Peninsula: Tōyō Imin Kaisha (Orient Emigration Company) and the Hiroshima Imin Kaisha (Hiroshima Emigration Company).

58. *Hattenshi*, I, 223.

59. On Miyazaki see his autobiographical *San-jū-san nen no yume* (A

thirty-three years' dream), 3rd ed. (Tokyo, 1943), esp. pp. 73–118; Yamaguchi Kōsaku, *Miyazaki Tōten ron* (On Miyazaki Tōten; Kobe, 1964), esp. pp. 29–36; Kuzuu, *Tōa senkaku*, III, 684–85; Nakajima, *Taishi kaikōroku*, II, 873–75; Jansen, *Japanese and Sun Yat-sen*, esp. pp. 57–58.

60. Ishibashi returned to Japan in December 1895. He was active in the Pan-Asian oriented *Seikyōsha* (Political Education League) in Tokyo until his death in March 1898 at the age of thirty. Kuzuu, *Tōa senkaku*, III, 47–49 ("Retsuden").

61. Miyazaki, *San-jū-san nen no yume*, pp. 86–88. On Surasag's clash with his less militant colleagues, his resignation as army commander, his subsequent appointment as minister of agriculture and his dislike of this non-military post, see his own account in *Prawadkaan*, IV, 265–69. On his financial problems see note 54 above.

62. The *shishi* who accompanied Miyazaki on this occasion included several individuals who later attained a certain measure of fame in the Chinese revolution as Pan-Asian agitators, particularly Hirayama Shū, Suenaga Setsu, and Miyazaki's own brother-in-law, Maeda Kyūnishirō. *San-jū-san nen no yume*, p. 105.

63. For Miyazaki's subsequent activities see *ibid.*, pp. 118 ff; Yamaguchi, *Miyazaki Tōten ron*, pp. 37 ff; Jansen, *Sun Yat-sen and the Japanese*, p. 59 ff.

64. Iwamoto's subsequent career is recounted in his *Jikki*, pp. 5 ff and 221 (of 1943 edition). In 1896 he made an arduous 111-day journey on foot from Bangkok to Hanoi in the company of Yamamoto Shinsuke, both disguised as yellow-robed Buddhist monks. Iwamoto's *Jikki* is a day-by-day journal of this "scouting trip" which took them through the treacherous jungles of Siam, Laos, and Tonkin and cost the life of Yamamoto, who died in Hanoi in 1897. The journey was certainly one of the most remarkable feats by Meiji activists anywhere. "Ironlegs" Iwamoto, as he thereafter dubbed himself, survived until 1920.

65. Wyatt, *Politics of Reform*, pp. 137, 160, 224, 330, 360.

66. Agawa, *Shamu ōkoku*, pp. 143–51; Amada Rokurō, "Shinkōbukai Nittai kankei" (Friendly Thai-Japanese Relations), MS (ca. 1962), unpag.; *Shinsen daijinmei jiten*, VII, 530, *s.v.* "Yasui Tetsuko."

67. *Shinsen daijinmei jiten*, VI, 108, *s.v.* "Masao Tōkichi"; Kuzuu, *Tōa senkaku*, II, 833–34.

68. Shamu Kyōkai, ed., *Shamu kokujō* (Conditions in Siam; Tokyo, 1929), pp. 228–30, 850–51.

69. Agawa, *Shamu ōkoku*, p. 150; Nan'yō oyobi Nihonjin Sha, ed., *Nan'yō go-jū nen* (Fifty years in the South Seas; Tokyo, 1938), pp. 140–41. For Inagaki's biography: Kuzuu, *Tōa Senkaku*, III, 37; *Shinsen daijinmei jiten*, I, 319.

70. *GK*, File 2-5-1, No. 17, Inagaki to Okuma, June 28, 1897, App. 1; Saionzi [sic] to Devawongse, June 25, 1896, attached aide memoire.

71. *Ibid.*, Inagaki to Okuma, June 28, 1897, App. 1; Saionji to Kirkpatrick, "Oboegaki" (aide memoire), June 25, 1896.

72. Texts of the treaty in *ibid.*, and in *British and Foreign State Papers*, XC, 66–72 (1897–1898).